Write Your Life Story

Brainstorm, Write and Publish Your Autobiography

Steve Alcorn

Books by Steve Alcorn

Write Your Life Story
How to Fix Your Novel
Writing Young Adult Fiction
Adapting Novel to Screenplay: Everything In Its Path
Theme Park Design: Behind the Scenes with an Engineer
Building a Better Mouse: The Story of the Electronic Imagineers Who Built Epcot
A Matter of Justice (a Dani Deucer mystery)
Everything in its Path (historical fiction)
Ring of Diamonds (writing as Sharon Stevens)
Travel Kid (a pictorial journal)
Orlando ABC (for children)
Molly Builds a Theme Park (for children)

e-mail the author at:
steve@alcorn.com

4th Edition

Theme Perks Press
themeperks.com

Table of Contents

Section 1 Your Life Story 1

Section 2 Structure 31

Section 3 Writing Tools 47

Section 4 Writing Prompts 77

Section 5 Your Manuscript   117

Section 6 Publishing Your Work   139

Dedication

To Dani, my favorite collaborator; and Linda, my soul mate.

Section 1
Your Life Story

Chapter 1

Welcome

Welcome to Write Your Life Story. I'm Steve Alcorn, theme park designer, author and online instructor. I'll be your mentor for this adventure into writing your life story.

I'm the author of many books, including a variety of fiction and non-fiction, and my own autobiography, *Building a Better Mouse*. It's about the Imagineers who created Epcot.

I'm also the editor of *Valentine's Day*, a memoir by Australian author Pamela Collins. It tells the story of her life on a tropical island during the 1950s.

These two biographies take completely different approaches, and illustrate how important it is to decide on your organization before you start writing. That's just one of the many topics we'll discuss in the coming chapters.

Whether or not you want to share your story with the public, or just your family members and future generations, this book will give you all the tools you need to create that story.

What's in this Book?

We'll begin by asking "Why write your life story?" That might seem like a silly question since you're already reading this book, but in fact it's a very important question, because your reasons for writing your life story will impact what you decide to put into it.

Then we'll also ask whether you want to write biography or autobiography. Instead of *your* life story you might be writing a life story of someone else you know, perhaps someone in your family, or an ancestor. No matter who you're writing about, it's going to influence the way you write. And if you write about yourself, you can also write about yourself either autobiographically or more biographically; I'll explain the impact of those choices on the way you write.

Next we'll discuss specific ways of getting your story down on paper—or recording it as audio or video—and how those choices impact the process.

What form your story will take? Will it be a journal, a blog, an article, a series of recordings, a collection of short stories or something resembling a novel? You could even create your story in a question and answer format.

I'll talk about tailoring your story to your audience. If you're writing for your friends and relatives your story might be different than if you're writing for future generations. And if you're writing to share your story with children, it might be different than if you're writing to share it with adults.

Are you going to stick just with the facts or are you going to fictionalize some aspects? There might be things you don't want people to know, or you might just want to spice things up and create something more exciting than everyday life.

I'll talk about do's and don'ts: things you should and shouldn't do as you write your life story.

After these introductory chapters we'll turn to the important topic of structure. The structure of your life story will be very different depending upon several choices you make.

Structure

There are three ways you can organize your story.

The first is *chronological organization,* where events are arranged from beginning to end in chronological order.

Another possibility is *thematic organization,* where related events throughout your life are grouped into separate thematic sections.

Finally, you can use *anecdotal organization,* to simply tell your story using... well, stories. That's a fun way to enlighten readers.

Writing Tools

Once you've figured out how you're going to organize your story we'll explore writing tools.

We'll talk about the difference between *plot* and *story*. We tend to use those terms interchangeably in everyday life but they're very different things. I'll explain the difference, and show you how, by balancing them, you can achieve maximum excitement and maximum emotional impact in your writing.

During high school you probably heard about Greek three-act structure. It's a great way to structure your story. I've developed an even more precise version for you that turns three-act structure into a series of nine checkpoints. Using this technique, you'll end up with a perfect dramatic structure for anything that you write.

You'll also make decisions about what viewpoint and tense you wish to write in. Both of those choices will affect your writing style and how your readers perceive you.

I'll also show you how to include dramatic dialogue in your work. Dialogue is really fun to read (and write), and can make the difference between a bunch of dull exposition and scenes that enthrall your readers.

Lively and vivid settings are an important part of bringing your story to life, too. They enable you to place your readers in the scene, just as you experienced it.

Writing Prompts

A major part of this book is helping you jog your memory, and then organize those thoughts. We'll have many writing prompts to help you recall important—and even unimportant but fun—events to include in your life story.

We'll talk about the value of looking at old photographs, recalling conversations, engaging in a question and answer session with a friend or relative, pursuing the backgrounds of your ancestors, recalling where you were on a certain date, exploring your childhood, the toys you played with, the possessions you treasured as you grew older, your pets and how they shaped your life.

You'll explore what it was like growing up, progressing from teenager to adult. We'll look at your accomplishments in life. If you're a spiritual person you'll want to include some of that in your life story as well. We'll recall holidays and special times you spent with friends or loved ones.

We'll look at the most romantic moments in life, and also the sadder ones, because that sort of drama very much belongs in a life story. It shows others how resilient we can be in life.

If you have children or grandchildren, you'll be able to share the joy they have brought to your life and the special moments you've spent with them.

Finally you'll revisit the changes you've experienced in the world, from technology to your own life's circumstances.

The Writing Process

Once you have all those memories collected, the writing process can proceed swiftly and smoothly using a technique I call *writing big*. It helps you bring maximum impact to every sentence, every paragraph and every page.

And once your manuscript is written, I'll show you how to polish it. This is about more than some dull editing process. I'll show you a few simple techniques that are actually fun and exciting, so you can easily improve your writing.

We'll also take a look at the fun topic of illustrations, and brainstorm what the cover of your book might look like.

And we'll explain how copyrights and permissions work, so that everything in your book is something you're entitled to use.

Getting Published

Once your work is ready, you'll be ready for publishing. I'll show you how to get it into print.

Whether you're writing your book for just a few family members or to sell to the public, you want to do the most professional job of publishing it. I'll also show you how to turn it into an e-book so it can be enjoyed on tablets and Kindles, and will never go out of print.

Of course, once your book is in print, if you wish to sell it to others, you'll need to market it. I have lots of great tips for how you can do that!

We've got a lot ahead of us, so let's get started!

Chapter 2

Why Write Your Life Story

Why Write your Life Story? This is not a rhetorical question! Only by fully understanding your *why* can you make informed decisions about *how* to write your life story and *what* you put into it. Some reasons may be obvious, but there might be some you haven't thought of yet.

Let me make some suggestions and you can see which ones apply to you.

One obvious reason to write your life story is for your family and friends to learn things about your past they may not know. It's not just about facts. It's a way for them to understand who you are as a person, and what made you the way you are today.

Another very good reason to write your life story is for future generations. These are people you may never know. Imagine how wonderful it would be if you could read the life story of one of your ancestors who lived 100, 200 or even more years ago! Well that's what you're doing for your descendants now, and it's a wonderful gift.

Another good reason to write your life story is to express your passion for something. If you feel passionate about a cause, about a person, about events in your past—record them so that everyone who reads your story can also feel that same passion. If you write with passion, readers will feel it.

Similar to passion, is theme. When I write I try to convey a message in the form of a theme. Your theme could be about overcoming adversity, learning a lesson, or the power of love. Incorporating a theme in your writing can convey a deeply meaningful experience to your readers.

Finally, it's wonderful to write your life story to inspire others. If you have experienced events from which you drew inspiration during your life or if your life struggle itself is inspiring, pass that on to others so they can see how you triumphed over adversity, how you lived through changes and how you found the inspiration to become who you are today.

What are your reasons for writing your life story? Which ones really struck home with you?

Once your manuscript is done, you might like to revisit this list, and see whether you've accomplished those goals. Then you'll know you've truly created something special.

Chapter 3

Biography or Autobiography

When writing a life story, you might think "Well of course it's an autobiography because it's about me". But you might want to write the story of someone close to you, someone in your family, or an ancestor. In that case you're writing a biography.

There is one other possibility, though. You might indeed be writing your own story but you could write it as a biographer would, from a third person viewpoint rather than intimately writing about yourself. This allows you to establish a certain distance from the subject, and interpret events with an impartial eye.

The difference between a biography and an autobiography is really the stance the author takes.

In a *biography*, the author is outside of the subject, watching what the subject does and interpreting those actions.

In *autobiography*, the author is the person telling the story; the author is inside the subject, telling us exactly how the subject feels.

Let's look at the advantages and the disadvantages of both.

Biography

In a biography, you have the advantage of a little bit of distance. You can leave certain things ambiguous, you can omit things the subject knew. You can also invent a few things that are unknown. For example, you could invent conversations that involved an ancestor. You weren't present to hear them, but as long as those conversations are believable and relevant, they help bring the story to life. No one is going to complain that it isn't exactly what was said, because they weren't there either.

The disadvantage of biography is that you can't ever quite get your readers to *become* the subject. Since they can't get inside the subject's head, they can't feel as if they have become the subject; they can only be spectators. It's the difference between watching a movie about someone and actually being that person.

Autobiography

Now let's look at autobiography. The advantage of autobiography is exactly the opposite; you're inside the subject's head. Everything they are feeling, you're feeling; everything they're experiencing, you're experiencing.

In an autobiography, readers expect conversations to be extremely accurate, because you are in a position to know. You were there, you experienced it, so you should record it as accurately as possible. That doesn't mean readers expect you to have total recall about every single word; but it does mean they expect accuracy in what you report.

The disadvantage of autobiography is that since readers *become* you as they read, they will learn your secrets, the most intimate details of your life. It's difficult to pull back and separate yourself from that.

You have to decide how much you want to reveal before you start writing, so the reader doesn't suddenly feel like you're pulling back and not revealing things. Don't introduce topics you're unwilling to thoroughly explore.

Now that we've explored the advantages and disadvantages of biography and autobiography, which will you choose?

Chapter **4**

How to Write Your Life Story

In this chapter we're going to look at how you're going to actually write your story—not all the nuts and bolts, but just in general how you go about writing your life story.

Make it Significant

How do you decide what you're going to write about?

You need to write about things you care about because readers want to learn about things that are important to you.

No one wants to read about the minutia of everyday life—watering the plants or driving the kids to school every day. The houseplants you're taking care of might be important to you, those kids are certainly important to you. But not to readers.

On the other hand, the joy and sadness of taking those kids to school on their first day of class is something both you and your readers will find important.

One way to determine what you should put into you life story is to read some other life stories. The topics you find interesting in those people's lives are the same things that will be interesting in your own life.

Many biographies are not about emperors who invaded Rome. They are about everyday people who had meaningful lives and wrote about things they cared about. Turn to them for inspiration.

A good example is *The Double Helix* by James D. Watson, one of the discoverers of the structure of DNA. The book is about a perfectly normal chap who stumbled onto an idea others around him had missed.

Make it Real

When you write about something, bring it to life; bring meaning to it. Don't just mention a topic, *explore* the topic. Don't just say "I drove the kids to school." Describe the car, describe the school. But describe them in ways that show you care about those things and that they were important. Bring them to life and make them vivid so we can experience them along with you.

Your Writer's Notebook

Now, it's time to start getting organized. I'd like you to begin by setting up a writer's notebook. It could be a physical notebook, or, if you're a computer person like me, create folders on your computer and call them your writer's notebook. Think of this as an idea book for you to keep track of all of the different ideas you want to include in your life story. I guarantee you'll encounter many in the coming chapters!

Whether it's a physical notebook or a set of files on your computer, you'll divide it up, with one section for each chapter topic in this book. Within those tabs or file names you'll have space for all that you're going to discover in the coming chapters.

Feel free to create other sections, as ideas occur to you. The organization doesn't matter right now, it's capturing ideas that's important.

You can create sections where you keep track of important dates. You can list people you want to make sure that you include. You can list events. Create a section for random thoughts, as well. Those random pages will allow you to make notes of things that occur to you in the middle of the night. When you wake up with a great idea, jot it down.

As you go through the course you'll be creating new pages or new files for each topic we talk about. Later, when you start writing your manuscript, you'll refer to these pages. You can rearrange them, organize them, and check ideas off as you use them. Since it's all right there, jotted down ready for use, it will be like an idea store! A place you go for the next idea you'll write about.

Your writer's notebook reflects the most important goal of this book, which is information gathering, memory gleaning, idea sparking. And that's what we'll embark on next.

Chapter 5

Journals, Blogs, Articles, Recordings, Stories and Books

There are many different ways that you can tell your story. This chapter explores the most common choices.

Journals

Journals can be a resource, or your end product. Perhaps you've kept journals or diaries throughout your life, either occasionally or conscientiously. If so, you're lucky, because you've got a lot of resource material to draw upon.

Or maybe you're just starting to keep a journal. It can tell your life story from this point forward. The topics in the book will help you decide what to include.

Blogs

Blogs are an online form of journal. While they might seem like simply an electronic version of a traditional journal, they tend to feel very different. The reason is that blogs are designed to be read by others, entry by entry, as they are created. Unlike a written journal, they aren't intended to be "fixed up" later on. So you need to think carefully about each entry, and write it to stand on its own. You don't have the advantage of context, because your readers probably haven't started reading at the beginning.

Sure, you could write your life story as a series of blog entries about the past, perhaps adding a new one every day. That's an easy way to end up with a complete life story in bite size pieces. But it does have the disadvantage that you essentially end up publishing a first draft, rather than having a chance to rearrange and polish before publication.

A better use for blogs is to write about the present, like an online diary of each day. If you're young, your life story is happening around you right now; that's a good way to capture it. You can always edit it into something more cohesive in the future.

Articles

Another approach is to create a series of articles. You could publish those articles in a magazine, a local newspaper, or a community gazette.

If you choose to take this approach, each article needs to stand on its own. You'll want to apply the structuring techniques discussed later in this book to each one of those articles so that they each have their own self-contained structure. Each will be about a change; each will be about an event; each will have a theme.

One of the nice things about doing that is that you can then collect all of those articles at a later date and publish them as one complete volume.

Recordings

An easy way to create your life story is as a series of recordings. This captures your thoughts, and will provide source material for yourself and future writers.

You can make audio or video recordings. You can have another family member ask you questions, or have a conversation with them. The memory jogging techniques in the prompt chapters of this book provide lots of great ideas for things to talk about.

The weakness of this approach is that while it provides great source material, it probably won't create a very organized end product that could be published as it was recorded. You'll need to do a lot of editing to turn it into a polished end result.

Stories

You could also turn your life into a series of short stories. These are a little bit longer than a magazine article and have more of a fiction feel, because they really put the reader into the situation and then play out like a movie. Short stories can just be about one particular episode in your life.

Books

The best life stories are complete books. They give readers time to really get to know the subject.

But even when writing a book, you don't have to start on the day you were born (or the day your great, great grandfather was born!) and go right up to the current moment. The book could focus on a particularly important period in your life. It could still contain memories from earlier times, without being exhaustive.

***

All of these different ways of telling your story are valuable, and serve different purposes. You may wish to employ more than one of them during the process.

For example, while you're putting together your material you can keep a daily blog. You can record reminders and interviews as video or audio. And then you could turn all of that material into a book. And then you can submit a chapter of that book as a magazine article.

Chapter

6

Tailoring Your Story to Your Audience

Who are your target readers?

They could be your children, your grandchildren, your parents, your grandparents, your friends, or they could be the general public. They could be all of the above. Or you might have a specific audience in mind for your book.

You need to answer this question at the outset so you can tailor your book to them.

Writing for Different Age Groups

A good example of tailoring your book towards your children and grandchildren is Charlton Heston's *To Be a Man*. His goal was to pass on to his grandchildren thoughts about what he felt manhood was, what was important to him, and how men should behave.

If younger readers are part of your target audience, you must use language that can be understood by them. Focus on topics they can relate to in their own lives. But avoid writing down to them.

If you're writing for an adult audience of family and friends you can talk about anything you'd like. But if you're writing for public distribution it is wise to filter out details you or those close to you might not want widely known. Even if you're writing for family members, there might be some things about your own life you don't want to share.

Themes

Once you know who your readers are you need to decide what sort of theme you wish them to take away with them when they finish reading your book. There are a *lot* of really great themes. Some of my favorites are:

Being Accepted and Meeting New People

All of us value being accepted when we move into new social groups. This has particular relevance if you write about your childhood and teenage years.

Discovering Talent

This is a great coming of age theme. What are you good at and how did you find that out? Did you ever think about being something other than what you are? And how did you decide that you were better at what you do now than what you did then?

Overcoming Challenges

This theme is one of the most prevalent in autobiographies. People love to read about conflict. Conflict is a major driver in fiction and there is no reason why it can't drive biographies and autobiographies as well. It's inspiring to write about challenges you faced (especially those you thought to be insurmountable) and you overcame them.

Civic Responsibility

This is a pertinent topic, particularly for younger audiences, where civil responsibility is stressed in school and volunteerism is encouraged. Everyone has to make choices in their lives - none of them more important than balancing one's personal needs with the overall well-being of the community. Showing how you were civically responsible can be very inspiring.

Learning to Love

A theme as old as mankind, falling in love is the easy part but handling the associated responsibilities is a lot tougher. What does it really mean to be in love and what are your duties when you're in love with someone? If the love falls apart or they die, how do you deal with that? These are topics that are painful to write about, but they define you as a person. Even though difficult, those experiences should be relived in order to write about them as authentically as possible.

Family

Family is important to almost everyone, whether child or parent. Writing about the importance of family is particularly meaningful if your life story is mainly intended for your own family members, but it can also resonate with the general public.

Naivety

Lots of characters in fiction, especially younger characters, are naive. Most of us have been naive at some point in our lives. So writing about naivety and how you overcome it is something almost everyone can relate to.

Forgiveness

Learning to forgive can be difficult. We've all been in situations where we carried a grudge longer than we should have, often for reasons that don't stand the test of time. Learning to forgive is an important gift we can pass on to others by writing about it.

Honesty

One way to illustrate the value of honesty is by sharing personal experiences where we might have been a wee bit dishonest, and the often humorous corners we managed to paint ourselves into. Conversely, it is uplifting to read stories about being honest when we expected the worst, and were pleasantly surprised by the outcome.

Prejudice

This can be a powerful theme, especially if you're older and you lived through times when prejudice was an accepted part of life. Whether you experienced prejudice or overcame it, it's important to write about it honestly.

Sacrifice

Individuals who make sacrifices are sympathetic subjects. Have you made a sacrifice in your own life? Was it worth it?

Dealing with Change

This book was created using technology that hadn't even been dreamed of a mere 15 years ago. Many changes have occurred in all of our lives and we've had to learn to deal with them. What did you like? What did you not like? Did you travel, relocate, get married, break up, come out, change religion, have a health crisis, or make a major lifestyle change? All of these things require constantly inventing new ways to adapt. Often very funny stories arise from the misunderstandings brought about by change.

Self-Worth

Discovering our value is a powerful topic. Most of us have messed up at one time or another. Then we've had to climb back out of that hole and rediscover our self-respect again. If you've been in such a scenario don't be bashful write about it. Show your readers that just because they are down one day doesn't mean they can't prevail the next.

Self-Confidence

One of the most universal themes in literature, and the most common flaw to give to a character in a novel, is a lack of self-confidence. If you faced that doubt and found a way to do something against all odds, it creates an inspiring story. Alternately, if you have an over-abundance of confidence you most likely are in politics and don't have time to write a book anyway!

***

Now it's time to visit your writer's notebook and jot down any themes that resonated with you. You'll want to convey at least one of them in telling your own life story, and the more you can relate to, the more you'll have to write about.

We're almost done with the planning phase! Next we'll examine the all important do's and don'ts of the writing process.

Chapter 7

Do's and Don'ts

This chapter shares some do's and don'ts as you write your life story. Let's start on a positive note, and begin with the do's.

Do Keep Up That Writer's Notebook

Your writer's notebook is your new best friend! Stuff it full of notes about your ideas including everything you think you should put in your book, and—just as important— things you should leave out. Keep it with you and jot down your insights as they come to you. The order doesn't matter. Just get them all captured in one spot.

Do Write Every Day No Matter What

It is critically important for all writers to write every day. Set aside a time, sit down at that time uninterrupted and *write,* even if it's only for half an hour. It doesn't matter if you don't feel inspired, if you have no ideas, or if you feel like you've got writer's block (incidentally there's really no such thing, there's just writing and not writing). Whatever the case, sit down and write. If it produces pure garbage you can always purge it later. But the odds are that even if your first five minutes of effort stink, you will produce something of value before you are done.

Do Save Your Work

Always save your work! No matter how much self doubt you are temporarily indulging in, don't throw *anything* away. Don't delete those files, and don't tear those pages out and throw them in the trash, however satisfying it might be to crunch the paper up into a really, really tight ball and hurl it across the room at maximum velocity. There's always some little nugget in there you can dredge up later on and use.

Also, save backups. Copy your work to a USB key or sign up for a Dropbox or iCloud or Google Drive account and let it sync to all your working folders. Dropbox will even let you retrieve deleted versions if you accidentally make edits you didn't intend.

Do Collaborate

There's no need to keep this project a secret! Support from friends and family members is amazing. They will naturally ask you about your progress, thus providing an incentive for you to keep at it.

More importantly, they can act as a sounding board for discussing the ideas you've had and the ideas you've rejected. They can give very constructive feedback about what they find interesting, what they'd like you to elaborate on and elements that are just getting in the way of your overall story. You'll be amazed at the results you can collectively achieve!

Do Pick Good Collaborators

A good collaborator needs to be responsive, honest and supportive. They should be able to provide criticism in a constructive fashion with an eye to making the work better and not tearing you down personally. But let's face it, we all know some folks who find fault with most everything. Be smart and do not invite them to participate. Just tell them the work is in the preliminary phase and not ready for review.

Do Be Honest

The quality of your work will be directly proportional to your personal honesty. If something is simply too painful either to you or to your potential readers, you can leave it out, but do try to be as honest as possible.

When you write about a rough subject, don't lie about it, don't fudge about it, and don't try to pretend your life was all rosy. Nobody has an entirely rosy life, and people want to read about (and learn from) the hard times as well as the good. Even if it's painful for you to revisit some of those memories, it will be worth it. Working through them will make you feel better and seeing how you worked through them will inspire others.

Now for the don'ts…

Do Not Start Without a Plan

The cardinal rule for all forms of writing is *do not start without a plan.* Do not be a *pantser.* Pantsers are amateurs who write "by the seat of their pants."

If you blindly start on page one and are inspired to write really beautiful prose you will peter out in short order, since you have no idea what direction to go next. It might take a paragraph, it might take a page, it might even take a chapter, but peter out you will. And then you will get discouraged and you will stop and you will give up. So don't do that. Having the discipline to create a structure up front guarantees you can get to those magic words "The End."

Do Not Recite Events (Boring!)

Don't recite events. You're writing your life story, not a telephone book. It does not have to be a mind numbing list of things that happened (on October 22 I had a Whopper at Burger King). Yawn. That is not a life story, that is an event. You need to group things in ways that make sense.

We'll talk about different ways things can be grouped and how to select the important events in later chapters. You need to fully engage your readers so they experience the place and time through your eyes. Let it come to life with dialogue and action that imparts a theme and makes readers feel like they've lived your life.

Do Not Edit As You Go

For all forms of writing it is important to not edit as you go. If you try to polish your prose paragraph by paragraph, sentence by sentence, you are doomed to failure. If you are constantly reading back everything you have written, you will never get to the end.

When writing the first draft the overall flow is much more important than linguistic perfection. Your goal should be to get to the last page. Then you can go back and start polishing things.

We'll cover all the tools you need to do that polishing later, but it's important to maintain momentum for now. So just plow through and keep writing as you follow your plan to the end. Only then should you start dealing with the typos and tweaking of your sentence structure.

Do Not Become Discouraged

Do not get discouraged, even if the going sometimes gets tough. You have all the tools at your disposal to succeed. Start this project with a positive attitude. From the moment you write your first sentence you have already written one more sentence about your life than anyone who never started. And each new sentence adds one more step towards conveying your life to other people. Think about all the things you've accomplished already in your life and how great it will be to share your story. Stay positive and you will end up with something fantastic.

On that uplifting note we are going to advance to the nuts and bolts of writing: story structure. Now the fun really begins…

Section 2
Structure

Chapter 8

Fact or Fiction

Are you writing fact or fiction?

Fact means you're sticking with "the facts, ma'am, and nothing but the facts." It means everything you put down is absolutely true and you've omitted very little, certainly not enough to mislead.

Fiction means you've taken certain liberties with what's happened. For example, inventing conversations may cross the line from fact to fiction, depending upon whether or not you had a similar conversation.

Perhaps you've invented events that didn't really occur, but that represent what could have occurred, and which logically led to what actually followed. This is a fictional technique, often used in biography, where the biographer has no idea whether or not the events really occurred.

If you've invented things, then when you're writing biography—and certainly if you're writing autobiography—you need to include a note, perhaps on the title page, that says some of the events have been fictionalized for dramatic purposes.

There is no problem doing that if you think it creates a more dramatic work. But if you're trying to convey what your life was really like to others it may not be the best choice.

Artistic License

Your Artistic License entitles you to do anything you want.

Particularly when writing fiction, you have free rein.

But even when writing non-fiction, you can take some liberties. If you don't remember exactly what someone was wearing, you can invent what they were wearing—if it's in style with their character.

But you must be careful. The disadvantage of taking artistic license with events that people presume are true is that you could open yourself up to libel.

Fiction authors avoid this problem by including boiler plate text on their title page that says something like:

> This is a work of fiction. Names, characters, businesses, places, events and incidents are either the products of the author's imagination or used in a fictitious manner. Any resemblance to actual persons, living or dead, or actual events is purely coincidental.

Of course, you could turn your life story into fiction if you're willing to change your name and the names of all the characters.

My friend Pamela Collins wrote a terrific book that is pretty much an autobiography about her youth. She titled it *Valentine's Day,* after the name of her father in the book, Valentine. But that wasn't really his name. In fact, the names of every single character—including herself—have been changed.

Is that book fact or is it fiction? It reads as fiction, and it's even couched with a ghost appearing at the beginning to help tell the story. So readers don't really expect any of the events in the book to be exactly accurate. However, if you know Pamela you might suspect that most of them are pretty true!

So that is an advantage of using your artistic license. By changing all of the names and the settings you liberate yourself from any libel concerns and can do what you like.

But in general, if you're writing biography or autobiography you really can't credibly include that notice because everyone is going to know that much of it is based on truth. This would be a more appropriate notice:

> I have tried to recreate events, locales and conversations from my memories of them. In order to maintain their anonymity in some instances I have changed the names of individuals and places. I may have changed some identifying characteristics and details such as physical properties, occupations and places of residence.

When I'm writing autobiography, I want to stick absolutely to the truth. I want people to know that this is—to the best of my recollection—just how it happened, so they can experience it the way that I did.

But that's a decision you need to make for yourself. And you should make it now, before you proceed to the organization stage.

Chapter **9**

Chronological Organization

In this chapter we're going to talk about the first of three different possible ways you can organize your life story, chronological organization. Chronological organization means arranging events in the order they occurred, from beginning to end.

You don't necessarily need to start with the creation of the universe, or even your birth. You can start wherever you like and end wherever you like. But the events in between should be arranged in chronological order, from the beginning to the end of that part of your life.

Choose a part of your life when something dramatic happened. It should be a period of change—ideally not just external change or changing circumstances, but also internal change, a period when you overcame a flaw to become a different person.

We all go through many such changes in our lives. Think about situations where you evolved into a new version of yourself as a result of events. That's a very interesting thing to write about.

Just because you've selected one part of your life, it doesn't mean you can't include memories, conversations, or flashbacks about earlier periods, even though your story is in chronological order. You can incorporate them as memories, or in dialogue. But the general organization of the "now," the time you're describing, should be chronological.

A good example is George Burns' wonderful autobiography *Gracie: A Love Story*. It's about his beloved wife, Gracie Allen. He covers the events of their lives in chronological order. But he doesn't start with his birth and he doesn't end at the time he wrote the book, when he was almost a hundred years old. Instead he begins when he met Gracie; that was the beginning of a life-changing period. He goes through their history together, how their careers built, and how they got into television. The book ends with Gracie's death. That's a perfect example of chronological ordering.

What is the disadvantage of chronological ordering? If the part of your life you're describing is brief, it will leave us wondering what happened before and after. George Burns didn't have that problem, because he was with Gracie for much of his life.

Chronological organization is your best choice if the most important thing that happened in your life took a little while and is completely encapsulated in one chronological period. If your life is more… shall we say, episodic… then there might be other, better ways to organize your story. We'll look at another technique in the next chapter.

Chapter 10

Thematic Organization

Thematic organization is when you pick different events in your life and arrange them to form themes. In this approach the story is no longer chronological, but instead is grouped by topic, so that different related events are gathered together, perhaps in a single chapter.

For example, if you had many pets, you could talk about all of them in one chapter. If you had multiple marriages, you could talk about your different marriages in one chapter. Another chapter could be devoted to children. And yet another could be about your ancestors. And so on.

There are also other ways to arrange things thematically. A great example is a book by comedian and musician Kinky Friedman. It's quite touching compared to most of his humor. It is called *Heroes of a Texas Childhood.* It's not exactly autobiographical, because it's about heroes he had when he was a kid. You learn a lot about Kinky Friedman from the stories he chooses to tell about these people. There is a different person featured in each chapter, and the theme of each chapter arises from an experience that person had. One of them dealt with prejudice, many supported various liberal causes, and a number of them faced adversity and had to overcome it. It's a collection of little biographies, but when you put it all together the overall theme reflects the topics Kinky Friedman feels passionate about. It's a very original way to organize a combination biography/autobiography.

The advantage of thematic organization is that readers are likely to come away feeling strongly about topics you feel strongly about.

The disadvantage is it's much tougher to convey an impression of who you are without any kind of a chronology. They will appreciate certain facets of you based on the themes you choose, but they may not get an entire picture of your life or who you are as a complete person.

When I was in the eleventh grade we had an experimental textbook about American History that was arranged thematically rather than chronologically. It took me years to recover from that and grasp the true sequence of events!

It's possible to combine the techniques of chronology and theme. If you like some things about chronological organization and you like some things about thematic organization, don't rule out one or the other, you could use both. In your writer's notebook make a note of the things you might treat as themes in your book and then you'll be able to see whether or not you can also combine those with a chronological approach later on.

In the next chapter we'll turn our attention to the third way of organizing your life story, which is anecdotal. And it's even possible to combine this with your chronology and themes!

Chapter **11**

Anecdotal Organization

The third way you can organize your life story is anecdotal. Anecdotal means telling short, amusing stories. This is a good way to organize your life story if you aren't trying to convey the entire chronology of your life, and if you don't have any strong themes you want to express.

This technique is well used by George Burns in *One Hundred Years, One Hundred Stories*. He tells one hundred true stories about his life with Gracie and their performing career. They're not arranged in any particular order and they don't convey any particular theme. But they are very entertaining. When taken as a whole, the stories do give you a pretty good picture of who George Burns was as a man and as an entertainer, even though you would not be able to put together a complete chronology of his life and even though you might not be able to determine too many things he was passionate about.

It is possible to take this approach and combine it with the previous chronological and thematic approaches, so that themes are expressed in anecdotes and arranged chronologically.

Ernest Hemingway did this in *A Moveable Feast*. It's a memoir of his time in 1920s Paris as an American ex-patriot, and his adventures with interesting people like F. Scott Fitzgerald. The book consists of a series of anecdotes that take place more or less in chronological order and that express the theme of what a wild and creative time it was for

American ex-pats in Paris during the 1920s. It's an amalgam of all three of the organizational techniques we've talked about so far.

***

So consider all three of these organization techniques. Make some notes in your writer's notebook about which one of these would work best or which combination would work best. Perhaps you can devise a way to use all three in your writing.

Once you've decided upon structure, in the next chapter we're going to take a look at the different types of biography and autobiography you can write.

Chapter 12

Types of Life Stories

In this chapter we're going to take a final organizational look at your overall approach before we work on the structural underpinnings. This is where you need to decide what type of life story you are going to write. These are your choices:

Biography and Autobiography

You can write a biography or an autobiography. That is essentially the story of a person's life during most of their lifespan. You need to tell where they came from and where they ended up.

Memoir

You could also write a memoir. Ernest Hemingway's *A Moveable Feast* is a memoir because it is just a brief snippet of time, not the entire life of Ernest Hemingway. My own book, *Building a Better Mouse,* is a memoir because it describes a period of only about one year when we were constructing Epcot Center at Walt Disney World. A memoir has a beginning and an end, but it is not an autobiography of an entire life.

Family History

You could also write a family history. This is the biography of many different people all combined in one book. A family history is a great resource that many family members will enjoy, but it's not necessarily always exciting. You need to work extra hard in order to make the lives of all of those people come to life, so it's not just a recitation of events. You must bring the ancestors to life, show where they came from, what changed them, and how they ended up. It's much more work than writing one biography because it's writing many biographies; even if they're shorter, they still need to contain all the same things.

Confessional

Another form of life story is the confessional. These are sometimes difficult to write, particularly if you're sharing it with family members, because it involves baring your soul and revealing facts they may not know. You need to think very carefully about whether or not you want to do that before you start.

Meditation

A life story can also be a sort of meditation about life. This is a play on the theme concept; the same theme runs through the entire story. You need to be careful that it contains not just rumination, but also enough events to make it exciting, fun and interesting.

Essay

Your life story might be presented as an essay. This usually works best as an article or a blog entry. In an essay you will do more "telling" than "showing." You have a particular point you want to make. You introduce it and then add facts from your life to back it up. Then you sum up in a conclusion similar to the opening. This form of life story is a bit like writing a college essay, but it's about some things that happened in your life. Again, you have to work extra hard to make it interesting, so people want to read it; otherwise it might seem like you're preaching.

Travelogue

Travel essays, travel logs, and travel books are all very popular. I wrote one called *Travel Kid*. It's a collection of anecdotes about different places we visited when my daughter was growing up. Travel books are really fun to read if you're a traveler yourself. Make sure interesting things happen. Stories about people experiencing new cultures for the first time are fun.

Humor

Speaking of fun, the most fun type of life story is humor. Writers such as Dave Berry are extremely good at this style.

I find it difficult to write humor. It's hard to write something that is consistently funny and yet factual. If you're good at it I encourage you to do it, because the world needs more good humorists.

***

So there you have a list of all the different types of life story you might write. It would be hard to blend most of these types, so you really need to decide which one of these you're going to work on.

The tools and techniques that follow in the rest of this book apply to all of these different types of life story. But once you actually begin structuring and deciding what you're going to include, you're going to be somewhat locked in to the particular style you select.

So pick one of those now and then meet me in the next section. I'll see you there.

Section 3
Writing Tools

Chapter 13

Plot vs. Story

Let's begin our exploration of writing by taking a look at one of the most important concepts in all of storytelling; the difference between plot and story.

These are two words we use almost interchangeably in day to day speech, but they actually have very different meanings. Once you understand the difference between them, it's like a light bulb going off. You'll be able to write with much more impact, and much more emotion.

Plot is your physical journey. It is where you go and what you do.

Story is your emotional journey. It is how you changed inside, typically to overcome some sort of a problem.

An easy way to think of it is that *plot is action* and *story is reaction.* When something happens, that's plot. When you react to it, that's story.

Everything external is plot and everything internal is story. Actions, conflict, setbacks, and disasters are plot. Thoughts, feelings and decisions are story.

As you write, plot reveals what is seen, while story reveals the unseen. Plot is everything that happens, story is everything inside you.

Show, Don't Tell

You've probably heard the admonition, "Show, don't tell." It's much more powerful to *show* something happening than to *tell* us it happened.

If you *tell* us a book is on the table, that's not very interesting. But if you *show* us a person setting the book on the table, that's more interesting. That's how to *show* us the *plot*.

Similarly, if you *tell* us you felt sad, that's dull. But if *show* us that you shut yourself in your room for days without speaking to anyone, that is involving. That's how to *show* us the *story*.

You want to reveal both plot and the story through showing, not telling.

As you write, keep the concepts of plot and story clear. Describe exciting events, and then reveal the emotions they caused. It will make your writing much more vivid.

In your writer's notebook, as you record events, be sure to also jot down how you felt about them. That way you will be balancing plot and story. You'll be better prepared to write your manuscript because it will all be laid out in your writer's notebook: the physical plot, the emotional story.

Chapter 14

Story Structure

This chapter is vital. It gives you the structure you'll use to write your life story.

Three Act Structure

You've probably heard of three act structure. It's something the Greeks invented thousands of years ago. Most plays, books and movies are divided into three different acts, with rising tension starting in the first act and building throughout the second act until in act three, things reach a climactic point. And at that point there is a payoff and the audience experiences what the Greeks called *catharsis*, a relaxing of tension as a result of the climactic moment and the resulting reduced tension.

Checkpoints of Story Structure

I've taken three act structure and divided each act into three checkpoints, so nine total checkpoints. This makes it very easy to write any story. If you follow these nine checkpoints and keep them in order, I guarantee you will construct a successful and impactful story.

The length of these checkpoints varies dramatically. Some are very short, some could be very long. But what matters is the order. I'll discuss all nine of them in order and show you what goes into each one.

Act One

Act One begins with the **Hook**. This is something to get your reader's attention. You want to start *in medias res*. That means "in the middle of things." You want to start with some dialogue or some action. It doesn't matter whether your readers immediately understand what's going on, you want to hook them.

An important goal of the Hook is to introduce story questions to intrigue your readers, and keep them reading to find the answers.

The Hook might be only a few paragraphs or it could run for many pages. It doesn't really matter as long as your readers are intrigued and want to read on. That means you don't start with "I was born in," you start in the midst of something. Even if you're going to tell the story of your birth first, you can still start with some action or some dialogue, something about being born. Even if you just make up something that the nurses or doctors said, thrust us into the middle of the action at the very beginning of your story.

The next checkpoint is the **Backstory**. "Backstory" is a term used in literature that means everything that happened before the story began. That can certainly go into this checkpoint. But that sort of backstory could also be distributed throughout all three acts of a story, it's not necessary to put it all in this checkpoint. It's also not necessary that this checkpoint contain much true backstory. Its function is to fill readers in on the situation so they can interpret the Hook, and what comes later. But you definitely don't need to answer all of those story questions yet.

For example, if your Hook started with dialogue, the Backstory will gradually set the scene and reveal who is present, who they are talking to, and what the situation is. The Backstory can be a fairly long section, provided it's interesting and keeps us intrigued.

Act One ends with a very short checkpoint called the **Trigger**. This is something that directly attacks the main character (that's you in an autobiography) and the character's flaw. It doesn't have to be a huge dramatic event. It's not a Martian invasion, a declaration of war, or an attempted assassination. It's simply an event that is difficult to deal with because of the character's flaw.

For example, if your book is about dealing with adversity, at the beginning of the book you don't know how to deal with adversity, because you lack experience; perhaps you were naive, perhaps you lacked confidence, lacked self-worth. Whatever that flaw you had within you is going to change during the course of the story. The Trigger attacks that flaw. For example, if your flaw is lack of self-confidence, the trigger should challenge you to do something that you don't feel you can do. That leads you to Act Two.

Act Two

Act Two begins with a **Crisis**. It's the direct result of the Trigger. The crisis is a short internal moment where you are overcome by your flaw. So if you lack self-confidence, the crisis is simply that you are overcome by a lack of self-confidence, and can't do this thing.

This leads to the longest section in your story, the **Struggle**. The Struggle is the long, plot-heavy middle of your story. It could be more than half of the text. In it you will encounter many setbacks; it's the struggle of your life, before you changed. It is you attempting to come to grips with that flaw.

Sometimes you'll temporarily get the better of that flaw. Other times it may get the better of you. It is a time of setbacks and conflict, because you need to change. You must keep it interesting through conflict! If nothing interesting happens in the struggle, you will lose your readers. So things need to progress, you need to struggle against those obstacles that are thrown in your way, until you reach a very black moment. The black moment is where you are as low as you can go. It seems that all is lost, and there is no solution.

But then you have an **Epiphany**. It's a brief internal moment of insight, when you overcome your flaw. The epiphany is what readers read for. They've seen you struggling, they've known what is wrong with you, and they are rooting for you to change so you can solve your problems. And that's what happens in the epiphany.

Well, you don't solve them yet. But you realize what is wrong with you and you realize the need for you to change.

For example, if your flaw was lack of self-confidence then in the epiphany you realize you have lacked self-confidence throughout the struggle and you must change in order to be able to make a plan to solve your problem. You must believe in yourself.

Act Three

And that brings us to Act 3, which opens with a **Plan**. This is a plan you could not make until you overcame your flaw. A plan that you could not create without having changed.

The first plan may not work. You might have to make several plans. But one of them is going to work and it's going to lead you to the **Climax**.

The Climax is where you finally overcome the problem that you have been battling all this time.

A great technique in fiction writing is to have an antagonist who creates a lot of that conflict back in the Struggle. If you can identify an antagonist and overcome them in the climax, that's a very effective technique to show how much you've changed. It's also very effective to show that the antagonist is defeated because he failed to change.

But in life, things might not be so clear cut. We meet many antagonistic people, and it may not be easy to identify a single antagonist and defeat him in the climax. You just may need to overcome whatever the circumstances are in order to show that now you have truly changed.

Once the climax is done, you have arrived at the **Ending**. The dramatic tension of your story has evaporated. There's not very much left to do. So the ending section can't be very long. It needs to wrap things up quickly because you will lose reader's attention once they have seen that you have changed and solved your problem.

You don't want a long, rambling narrative here that tells what happened for the next however many years. You can intimate where things are going but you should leave it at that.

Applying the Checkpoints to Chronological Organization

These nine checkpoints will guarantee you a dramatically successful story. You might not be able to apply them to the entire course of your life but you can certainly apply them to some period of your life that had that dramatic structure. That will be a great read.

If you want to incorporate other details of your life that occurred before that, you can thread them in as backstory throughout all three acts. Your character can remember them or talk about them.

Clearly, this structure lends itself very well to the chronological organization we talked about earlier. It's ideal for a memoir. It's the way that I wrote *Building a Better Mouse*.

Applying the Checkpoints to Thematic Organization

This structure can also be used thematically. Each of your themes could contain a section organized in this way. For example, if a theme in one section is about overcoming self-confidence you can arrange it in this order. Then suppose another theme is overcoming prejudice. You can have another set of nine checkpoints showing that change. So you would have many sections, each with its own dramatic payoff. In fact, each could almost stand alone, like separate short stories.

Applying the Checkpoints to Anecdotal Organization

Finally, the checkpoint structure also works for anecdotal organization. Unless the anecdote is extremely short or just meant to be humorous with some sort of surprise ending, most good anecdotes also teach a lesson. They show how someone learns something. And that means they changed.

***

As you can see, you can apply this structure to any of the organizational forms we talked about and any of the life story formats that we talked about. It will serve you well in all of your writing, both biographical and fiction. It's the heart of all great storytelling. Use it well.

Chapter **15**

Viewpoint and Tense

In this chapter, we're going to look at two other important choices you're going to make in writing your life story. The first one is viewpoint.

There are many different viewpoints, but three of them are the most useful.

Omniscient

Omniscient means "all-knowing." As the name suggests, you're writing as an all-knowing author. You know absolutely everything, everywhere. You could say that a rock fell over on the planet Mars and two minutes later there was a tornado in Kansas.

The problem with Omniscient is that although it allows you to write anything you want, it creates a great distance between your characters and your readers. Sure, you can tell your readers what your characters are feeling, because you can dip into everyone's head. But readers won't really connect with any particular character. If your work is an autobiography it would be particularly awkward to write in Omniscient, because it would be like reading everyone else's mind.

Looking back on events, you may know much more about what happened than you did at the time, so omniscient *could* reveal facts you didn't know then, but that's not necessarily a good thing. If you want readers to "become" you as they read, it works better if they don't know anything you didn't know at the time.

So while magazine articles or scientific journals might work well in Omniscient viewpoint, it's usually not the best choice for storytelling, where you want to create a relationship between your main character and your readers.

Third Person Limited

Third Person Limited uses pronouns like "he" and "she" to refer to the characters—including your main character. In this viewpoint, you are not "I," you are "he" or "she." Any thoughts are restricted to the viewpoint character. The thoughts of all others are unknowable, except to the extent that—as in real life—you can interpret their actions or words.

Third Person Limited is a great choice for biographies. If you're writing about an ancestor or relative it will work great. But it's a bit artificial in an autobiography.

First Person

In an autobiography, you typically use the pronoun "I." That is, after all, the natural way we tell stories about ourselves.

First person has only one downside in this instance: it's very easy to create "I" strain. That's when every sentence begins with the word I. "I did this" and "I did that" and "Then I did this." It becomes very tiresome. You need to mix up the sentence structure and find a more interesting way to phrase some of them. For example, instead of writing "I arrived at the train station," just say "The train station was dark and dingy." We'll get the idea that you must be there or else you wouldn't be describing it.

***

That brings us to your choice of tense. There are several tenses, but only two that are particularly useful for storytelling: past tense or present tense.

Past Tense

Since you're telling the past story of your life, it's logical to choose past tense in your writing. You use verbs like "was" and "were" and "did" and the past tense forms of verbs like "ran" or "swam." That's a perfectly good way to tell your story and is probably the one you will select.

Present Tense

Of late, it has become stylish to write stories in present tense. A lot of fiction is being written in present tense. At first, it strikes one as a little odd, because it's not the natural way we tell stories.

When we tell someone what happened yesterday we say, "I met Joan yesterday and we decided we would go to a restaurant tomorrow." We don't say "I meet Joan yesterday." That makes no sense.

But you could say: "The day dawns bright. I rise, dress and walk to the market. On the way I meet Joan, coming from the other direction. We meet, we talk, we agree to go to a restaurant on Tuesday." That makes perfect sense, and it's present tense.

Although it may have seemed a little weird during the first sentence you quickly got used to it. And it has one advantage over past tense: present tense feels very immediate. We feel we are right there, and it is happening now. This gives your writing a great immediacy.

But it can be hard to stay in present tense, because we're not used to telling stories that way. So while you may wish to consider present tense as a viable way to tell your story, I certainly won't be surprised if you choose past tense. It is very common in autobiographies.

My Recommendations

So my recommendation for autobiography is first person, past tense. And for biographies, I recommend third person past tense. But I'd like you to experiment with all of the possibilities. Write a paragraph in each of the different possible viewpoints and tenses and see which one you think works the best for you. You might be surprised.

Chapter 16

Dialogue

In this chapter we're going to look at the all-important subject of dialogue. It's essential you use good dialogue to tell your life story. It's what brings your manuscript to life.

Without dialogue, readers will flip open your manuscript and it will be a solid page of gray exposition and it won't look interesting to read. But with dialogue, you'll break up all that exposition and bring it to life.

And dialogue doesn't just enhance readability. It serves many purposes. We'll begin by exploring the many uses of dialogue.

Then I'll have some pointers for how to format your dialogue so it's clear who is speaking and how they are speaking.

Finally I share a list of do's and don'ts that will help you write the very best dialogue so your story will have maximum impact and readability.

Let's start by looking at the many uses for dialogue.

Dialogue is Conflict

When people have a conversation about the weather, that's not dialogue, that's everyday conversation. You don't want that in your life story, it's boring.

Dialogue is a form of conflict. That's its primary use.

When there's dialogue in your life story, somebody wants something and somebody else is trying to avoid giving it to them. Somebody has a goal and the other person is opposed to that goal. That's the main purpose of dialogue in your manuscript.

Dialogue Conveys Emotion

Another purpose of dialogue is to convey emotion. Rather than tell us how people feel, you can show us how they feel by having them talk about it.

Dialogue Advances the Plot

An important purpose of dialogue is to advance the plot. Without dialogue, many things would never happen. If someone has a goal to convince someone else to go along with them, they have to convince them of that goal. Dialogue moves the action forward. Plot is action, and dialogue is the grease on the axles of that action.

Dialogue Sets the Scene

Dialogue can also be used to set the scene. Instead of telling us about the scenery, let your characters talk about how beautiful the mountains are with their snow-capped peaks and their mantle of green pine trees. If you put it in dialogue, readers are more likely to pay attention, rather than skip over the description.

Dialogue Develops Your Character

Dialogue is a great way to develop your character. In everyday life we learn what people are like from the things they say. We learn about their personalities, their goals, their setbacks and their emotions. It works the same way in your writing. Use dialogue to develop the characters you meet in your life story. After all, that's how you learned about them in the first place.

Dialogue Replaces Exposition

Dialogue is a great way to replace exposition. Instead of saying "John and Sally argued about the color of the sofa," put the argument into your manuscript. It's action. It's a chance to develop their characters. And it's much more fun to read than exposition. Dialogue will bring the scene to life.

Dialogue Breaks Up the Narrative

Finally, dialogue just plain breaks up narrative. People will only read so many lines of text before they want to get to something someone says. Use dialogue to avoid boring your readers.

***

Now that we know the uses of dialogue, let's look at some techniques for using it.

Dialogue Punctuation

Dialogue can be a bit intimidating. All that punctuation. But it's really not that complicated. The usual practice is to put dialogue in quotes and place an attribution after it, separated with a comma inside the closing quote mark. The attribution will not be capitalized, because it's part of the same sentence:

> "Hello," he said.

The only thing that's a little weird is that if the quote is a question, you still don't capitalize the attribution, even though it sort of looks like you should:

> "How?" he asked.

That's really about all there is to dialogue punctuation. The other important rule is to change paragraphs each time you change speakers. This would be confusing:

> "Hello," he said. "How are you?" she asked.

But this isn't:

"Hello," he said.
"How are you?" she asked.

Attributions

Your readers need to know who is speaking. The most common way to provide that informations is with attributions such as "I said" "she said" or "he said." Those are useful —essential even—to help us keep straight who is speaking, particularly when there are more than two people in a scene.

You should establish who's talking at the very beginning. It's best to put "said" at the beginning of the first line of dialogue if it's more than a few words long.

I said, "Let's sit down and talk about this."

is clearer than:

"Let's sit down and talk about this," I said.

In the second case we have to read the entire line to figure out who is talking. This is particularly true with longer speeches.

With only two characters in a scene you don't need an attribution on every single line. Just insert them often enough to remind us who is talking.

But attributions can become tiresome. *Beats* can help relieve that.

Beats

A way to avoid too many attributions is to use *beats*. Instead of using "said," you can associate a simple action with the dialogue and readers will assume the person who performed the action is the one who spoke. For example:

I sat down. "What's for dinner?"

It's obvious the person who sat down is the one who asked what's for dinner. Or:

John put the empty candy dish back on the table. "Do you have any more of these?"

It's obvious John asked the question.

As long as the dialogue is grouped with a beat, it's easy to tell who is speaking. But this would be confusing:

> John put the empty candy dish back on the table.
> "Do you have any more of these?"

It's not clear who spoke because the dialogue is unattached.

Stage Action

Another technique related to beats is *stage action*. Stage action is just like a beat, but it's a little bit longer. Using a beat you might write:

> John put the empty candy dish back on the table. "Do you have any more of these?"

Stage action could consist of a whole collection of sentences about John going to the kitchen, rummaging in the cupboards, returning with the empty dish, and then speaking.

Multiple Speakers

It can become confusing when you have multiple people in a scene. Dialogue scenes are best when there are only two people. If more people engage in the exchange you'll need a beat or attribution on every line, or we'll get incredibly confused.

Imagine John, Mary, Stu and Amy are in a scene:

> "Hi," said Mary.
> "I'm glad you could come," said John.
> "When is dinner?"

Who said the last line: Mary, Stu or Amy? It's impossible to know.

If more than two people are in a scene, consider having some of them wander away while the conversation takes place between the two remaining. Then you don't have to worry about readers keeping track of more than two people. If that's not possible, you'll need an attribution or beat on every line, and if the speeches are long preferably at the beginning of the lines.

Broken Dialogue

In real conversations it is uncommon for people to speak in completely well-formed sentences that flow the way you would write them. People communicate in fragments, partial sentences, and interruptions.

> John picked up the candy dish. "What the—"
> "Oh, sorry. Forgot to refill that," said Mary. She took it into the kitchen.
> "Let me…," John began, but she was already gone.

It can be a challenge to make these exchanges sound real, so try reading your dialogue out loud after you've written it to see if it sounds like people talking. If it consists of a bunch of broken phrases and partial sentences, then it's probably good.

Dialect

Dialect used to be very much in style. Here's the first paragraph of Mark Twain's *The Adventures of Huckleberry Finn:*

> You don't know about me without you have read a book by the name of The Adventures of Tom Sawyer; but that ain't no matter. That book was made by Mr. Mark Twain, and he told the truth, mainly. There was things which he stretched, but mainly he told the truth. That is nothing. I never seen anybody but lied one time or another, without it was Aunt Polly, or the widow, or maybe Mary. Aunt Polly -- Tom's Aunt Polly, she is -- and Mary, and the Widow Douglas is all told about in that book, which is mostly a true book, with some stretchers, as I said before.

And that's one of the more readable passages! Here's the slave Jim's dialect:

> De bes' way is to res' easy en let de ole man take his own way. Dey's two angels hoverin roun' 'bout him.

You can't get away with that any more. Huck's speech is readable because it's mostly based upon word choices, but today's readers have no patience for the phonetic spellings of Jim's speech.

Misspelling words, dropped letters, and elisions should be avoided. Just suggest the speech with one or two words, and then use word order and choices to convey it. Rather than:

> "Ah ain' agunna tell yuh agin'," he said.

Try something like:

> "I ain't gonna tell you again," he said.

If you've described the character adequately, we can imagine the rest for ourselves.

Interior Monologue

Interior Monologue is when someone thinks in the same way they might speak. For example, if a character sees a mouse they might think, "There's nothing I hate more than mice."

By interpreting their thoughts as literal sentences you can sometimes make their thoughts more interesting than expressing them in exposition. This can be done in a number of different ways typographically. You could do it as actual dialogue with quote marks around it:

> "There's nothing I hate more than mice," she thought.

You can do it as italics:

> *There's nothing I hate more than mice,* she thought.

And sometimes you can just do it right in line, maybe as a separate paragraph:

> There's nothing I hate more than mice, she thought.

It even occasionally makes sense without the attribution. You can experiment with those techniques to see which works best for you. And it's fine to mix all of them in the same manuscript.

Non-Verbal Dialogue

A lot of dialogue isn't spoken at all. We communicate non-verbally much of the time. We grunt, we nod, we shrug our shoulders. Those are all effective methods of "speaking" without dialogue. You can use them to reflect the way your characters communicate.

Just Say "Said"

You do not need to use lots of synonyms for "said." Maybe your English teacher told you you should use "expostulated" and "exclaimed" and "cried" and so on, to keep your dialogue interesting.

Don't do it.

Those words look absolutely ridiculous to professionals.

"Said" is an invisible word; you can use it as much as you like and no one will even notice. It's just there to keep things straight. Most of its synonyms are absurd.

It is impossible to "laugh" dialogue or to "grin" dialogue or to "spit" dialogue. You cannot "sob" dialogue or "sniffle" dialogue or "scoff" it.

Try it. It doesn't work. You can't do it, so your characters shouldn't do it. If they do, they will come across as maniacs.

Sure, a character can sob, and then speak. But they can't sob their dialogue.

There are a few attributions other than "said" which *are* useful (and possible). These include "shouted" and"whispered." But even these can usually be inferred from context. For example, a line of dialogue ending is an exclamation point has been shouted, and needs no attribution at all.

You Don't Need Adverbs. Ever.

You do not need an adverb to modify your attributions. In fact, you don't need an adverb in your entire manuscript.

Adverbs are those words that have "ly" tacked on at the end. You do not need to add adverb after adverb onto the different attributions in order to indicate how the dialogue is said. Good dialogue speaks for itself. We can tell from the words how they were delivered.

This has become a trend, and it is disturbing. In Stephanie Meyer's *Twilight* you will find chapters with almost 200 adverbs tacked onto dialogue! If you go through and cross out the adverbs you'll discover the dialogue actually reads better without them. Those adverbs are dead weight. They're doing nothing.

Good dialogue should speak for itself. Don't explain it. If someone says something that sounds like they're cross, you don't need to say they were cross. You don't need to attribute it with "they said crossly."

Just write good dialogue and your readers will get get it.

Chapter 17

Settings

You've probably been to many different places. Writing your life story presents you with the opportunity to capture those different places and transport your readers to them. Vivid settings can make the difference between a dull, boring manuscript and one that brings your story to life.

Let's examine the uses of settings in your manuscript, and some techniques for making them memorable.

Mood

Settings are one of the most powerful ways to establish the mood in your writing. Have you ever noticed in movies how when something sad happens the character walks in the rain? If something happy occurs, it's more likely to be sunny. Those are simple ways to use the weather to affect the mood.

Similarly, an expansive lawn creates a relaxed feeling (unless you have to mow it!) while dark woods create a feeling of foreboding.

Some places can be used to create two completely different moods, depending upon what details you choose to describe them. For example, a hospital waiting room can create anticipation for the birth of a child, or apprehension for the death of a loved one.

As you work on your life story, think about how the places where events occurred affected your mood at the time, and incorporate descriptions of them into your manuscript in order to recapture those moods.

Be Specific

The easiest way to sharpen a setting is to be specific. Rather than mentioning mountains in the distance, describe them as snow clad mountains wrapped in a girdle of green pine trees. Such details allow your readers to visualize your setting. In fact, providing a few specific details will encourage them to add details of their own that you didn't even mention.

***

Creating a Powerful Setting, Step by Step

I have a simple, step-by-step process I use to bring my settings to life. Starting with a very simple description of a place, I use this technique to build it up into something far more interesting. Here is how I do it, step-by-step:

First, as mentioned, add specific details.

Then create action within the setting. By "action" I don't mean this is a scene and the character is doing something. I just mean that no setting is completely static. Trees sway in the wind, cars pass on a street. I incorporate that action into the setting.

Next, add adjectives specifically selected to convey the mood. These aren't just any old adjectives like a "green" tree. They are adjectives that make a place seem gloomy, eerie, threatening, happy, hopeful, or whatever else the scene requires.

Then explore other senses, not just sight. Don't ignore any of the senses. Different settings have different smells. If you touch something, how does it feel? Is the temperature hot or cold? There are sounds everywhere in our world, what does your setting sound like? You can use adjectives to amplify those senses, too.

Add the potential for change. Almost no setting in this world is static; it doesn't just sit there. It changes with the time of day, it changes with the weather, it changes with the seasons. It changes as people use it in different ways. So add in the potential for those things to change even though we might be looking at the setting at a specific moment in time.

Then go through your entire setting and make sure you haven't used "was" or "were" as the verbs that describe your setting. It's very tempting to do so, but it's very passive. Find a more active way to phrase it.

For example, this is passive:

> There was an oak tree in the yard.

This is active:

> An oak tree grew in the yard.

Of course, both of those need a lot of work to make them truly interesting!

Finally, place your character—yourself, in an autobiography—into the setting. That way all of those senses become your character's senses. And because readers "become" the character as they read, they will experience it though their own senses.

Let's try this process out, step by step. We'll start with a simple setting and see if we can bring it to life.

> There was a path through the trees and into some bushes.

Now let's be more specific:

> There was a path through the trees and into a clump of bracken and spruce.

Let's create action, even in the inanimate:

> A path wound among the trees and into a clump of bracken and spruce.

We'll add adjectives that convey mood:

A path of matted pine needles wound among the trees and into a shadowy clump of bracken and snow-laden spruce.

Let's explore the other senses:

A path of matted pine needles wound among the trees and into a shadowy clump of bracken and snow-laden spruce. An icy wind carried the sharp tang of pine and the damp decay of the forest floor.

Add the potential for change over time:

A path of matted pine needles wound among the trees and into a shadowy clump of bracken and snow-laden spruce. An icy wind carried the sharp tang of pine and the damp decay of the forest floor. The swaying of the tallest pines indicated a change in the weather and more snow to come.

Use active verbs:

A path of matted pine needles wound among the trees. Fifty feet into the forest it disappeared into a shadowy clump of bracken and snow-laden spruce. An icy wind carried the sharp tang of pine and the damp decay of the forest floor. The tops of the tallest pines whispered of a change in the weather and more snow to come.

Finally, place your protagonist in the scene, and show it through her senses:

From her vantage at the edge of the forest, she could see the path of matted pine needles winding among the trees. Fifty feet in, it disappeared into a shadowy clump of bracken and snow-laden spruce. The icy wind reddened her cheeks, carrying the sharp tang of pine and something earthy, maybe the damp decay of the forest floor. High above, the wind swayed the tops of the tallest pines, whispering of a change in the weather and more snow to come.

See how the setting itself has became an active part of the story, creating a sense of impending change?

One of the best ways to develop effective settings like this is through the process of writing drafts. Your first draft may have a simple path through the forest, but by the time you finish, you should try to breathe life into each and every setting.

Now it's your turn. In your writer's notebook, take a simple setting, and apply the seven steps used above to bring it to life. They are:

1. Be more specific.

2. Create action, even in the inanimate.

3. Add adjectives that convey mood.

4. Explore the other senses.

5. Add the potential for change over time.

6. Use active verbs.

7. Place your protagonist in the scene.

***

In the next chapter we're going to begin our brainstorming sessions. You'll brainstorm the elements of your life story using a wide variety of prompts to jog your memory and inspire you. It's time to really start filling up that writer's notebook!

Section 4
Writing Prompts

Chapter 18

Photos

This is our first brainstorming chapter, where we go through different prompts to jog your memory and create entries for your writer's notebook. So make sure you've dedicated one page or one file to each one of these prompts and let's get started.

Photographs are a wonderful resource for jogging your memory. You probably have physical photo albums, shoe boxes full of photos, photos on your computer, photos in your phone, or all of the above. The good news is you don't have to organize them for this exercise. They'll become organized in your notes, but you can rummage through the photos however you like.

And as you look at each one, think about the situation it depicts, and whether it's something that would be interesting to readers, something that would help you describe your life.

It's obvious how photos can be a basic memory tool. But look deeper into those photos. Look for the details. Sometimes the objects, people or places in the background are the most important. They might tell the most interesting story.

Next, think about the backstory of that photo. How did your life carry you to that particular moment? How did the characters in that photo end up in that spot? What was happening? What conversations took place?

Suppose there's a house in the background. Where did the house come from? Who lived there? Are there stories about the house itself, how it was purchased or later sold? Does it remind you of other people, places, or things that you don't have photos of? Jot those down, too.

Don't put any limitations on yourself when you look at photographs. Jot down whatever leaps to mind, whether it's in the photo or not. And let the flow of memories carry you wherever it will. You've got plenty of time to get to the next photo once these ideas are all recorded.

Perhaps the event pictured isn't all that interesting, but something exciting happened in that spot later. Jot it down.

Perhaps the people in the photos did something interesting earlier, or later. Jot it down.

Perhaps an object in the photo had some past significance, or would become important later. Jot it down.

Once you've gone through your own photos, think about other photo resources. Just as you have collections, so do your family and friends. E-mail them and ask them to help you with your project by sending you photos they think would help.

Next, think about photos that might be publicly available. Google has a wonderful image search tool. Type in the places or activities you're interested in and you'll be amazed at the results. Some of them are bound to jog your memory. Of course you can't use the photos themselves in your story unless you get permission, but what's most important is using them as a creativity tool.

Set aside the photos you find most interesting for inclusion in your story if you decide to illustrate it. People love illustrated biographies.

If they're physical photos you can scan them into your computer (or have someone do it for you) so they'll be available when it comes time to assemble your story, a topic we'll discuss in a later chapter. And if the photos belong to someone else, ask them to send you written permission to use their photos so you can include those as well.

As you go through your photos, your notes will fall into many different categories, and you'll want a notebook section or file for each. What are these categories? They're the categories of the chapters that follow. So before you start looking at photos, read through the rest of this book, and create all those sections, filling them with whatever notes come to mind. Then it's time to look at photos.

If you're like me, you have a *lot* of photos. Don't let that overwhelm you. You don't have to go through them all at once. In fact, going through photos can be a fun break from the other brainstorming activities we'll explore in the coming chapters. So just go through a few at a time, taking notes, and then return to them later.

After a while you'll have notes on all the different prompt pages. And you'll be ready to move forward with organizing and writing your manuscript.

Chapter 19

Conversations

Recalling important conversations from your life and making notes about them creates a valuable resource for writing a life story.

In a previous chapter we discussed how dialogue provides dramatic conflict and character development. Conversations are quite different. Conversations are what take place in everyday life. You probably won't put a conversation verbatim into your life story. Most conversations tend to be about the weather. That's very boring.

But as you recall conversations that were pivotal moments in your life, extract the important details and turn those into dialogue that *will* be interesting to your readers.

But what about accuracy? How accurate do you need to be in reporting a conversation?

As long as you are not misrepresenting the conversation, there's no problem with being creative in interpreting *what* was said and *how* it was said to achieve the best dramatic effect. No one expects you had a tape recorder in your pocket to record every conversation you describe in your autobiography.

It's also fine to *invent* dialogue in scenes you didn't actually experience yourself, as long as it reasonably reflects what you understand occurred in those scenes.

A great resource for recalling conversations may exist in your media cabinet, or even on your phone. Old video recordings of yourself or your relatives or friends in conversation offer the possibility of a primary source. Even if the conversations aren't important, perhaps they will remind you of ones that were.

Just remember that when people are being recorded they often don't behave normally. They ham it up, or avoid controversial topics. But controversy is the very stuff that makes dialogue interesting. So you're probably going to have to rely upon your memory.

As you go through the writing prompts that follow, revisit the Conversations page of your writer's notebook whenever you encounter a topic that could best be portrayed using a bit of vivid dialogue.

For example, in the previous chapter we talked about the value of photographs as a memory jogging tool. If you see a photograph that depicts something that happened because of, during, or before some particularly heated argument or interesting verbal confrontation, that's some great dialogue that should be in your life story.

Chapter 20

Q&A

Question and Answer interviews are wonderful memory tools. Q&A is when one person asks questions and another answers them. It can be done in person, by telephone, by e-mail or even in written letters exchanged back and forth. The process of asking the question is the memory jogging tool.

Interviewing people who experienced important moments with you can be a valuable way to jog your memory and organize your thoughts. But what I'm really talking about here is not you interviewing them, but asking them to interview you!

It's best to select someone who knows at least a little bit about you and is interested in your life; they're best suited to thinking up the questions everyone would like answered.

During an interview you can use your smartphone to make a recording, but videos use up a lot of memory, and interviews can take many hours. So it's best to use a sound recording app; that way you don't need to worry about running out of storage.

Even if it's not possible to meet with your interviewer in person, you can still read the question aloud and record the answer.

I'm not the world's fastest typist, so I often make use of speech recognition software or online transcription services to turn my spoken words into written ones. It takes a bit of editing to create a professional end product, but it's a great way to generate a lot of manuscript pages very quickly. In fact, it's how I wrote this book.

But perhaps you're not a spoken-word type of person. If you feel more comfortable with the written word, you can type your answers. This has the added benefit that you're also creating material that can often be inserted right into your manuscript.

You could even post these answers as blog entries as you go along, and then compile them into your final manuscript when you're done. This is a great way to generate interest in your upcoming book. Think of it as advance marketing.

If you do the interview in person, keep a notebook nearby, even if it's being recorded. You can use the notebook to jot down topics that may not be germane to the immediate question, but might be interesting to include later. The question and answer session is both a tool for creating material and a tool for suggesting future questions.

Be sure to save your audio interviews. They'll make a great supplement to your life story. You can offer them online as a premium for those who buy your book, or even publish them as a separate audiobook.

Whether you do it in one face-to-face audio session or by an e-mail exchange that takes months, Q&A is a wonderful way to compile a tremendous amount of material that might not otherwise occur to you.

Chapter 21

Ancestors

Everyone has ancestors of course, but some of us don't know much about them. We may know who our parents and grandparents were, but as we try to go farther back in time it gets more and more difficult.

If it happened long ago, it's not really a part of your life, so do you need to include it? Perhaps, because it can provide a frame of reference to help readers understand who you are through discovering your origins. And of course if you are writing a biography of an ancestor you'll need to know all you can about them. In this chapter we'll look at some techniques you can use to find that information.

Of course if they're living you can ask parents or grandparents for details about your family tree. Or you can visit websites like ancestry.com where search tools provide a wealth of information to trace your ancestors. I was able to follow some branches of mine back to the 16th century!

Once you've found names, you'll be amazed how much other information turns up using web searches. Often you can even find related photographs of people and places.

It's also common to invent details from the distant past. If you're going back hundreds of years no one expects you to have precise details about what those ancestors did and said. It's perfectly acceptable to create imaginary scenes about those ancestors.

For example, did they emigrate to the New World? What would have been their reasons, their concerns, their conflicts and their surprises in doing so? You can't read their minds or see into the past, but you can capture the spirit of their lives in your imagination.

If you take this approach, simply include a brief statement, perhaps in a preface, that says you imagined it might have been like this. That way readers will know it's a fictionalized account of something that might have happened.

Family trees are complex. They have the unusual attribute of growing in both directions through time. As each person has multiple descendants and those decedents in turn have more, the tree broadens. But as you work your way up the tree, it also broadens, because each ancestor was the product of two people in the generation before.

It quickly becomes impossible to fit all of this information on one simple diagram, so be sure to take careful notes in your writer's notebook, and consider creating drawings to help you visualize the relationships. Sites like ancestry.com can help with this, by allowing you to print out different sections of your tree.

Have fun exploring! I hope you make some interesting discoveries.

Chapter **22**

Where Were You When

"Where Were You When" is a question technique to jog your memory. It's natural that we remember where we were when momentous events occurred, and summoning those memories can help us visualize the details of our lives at those times.

People of my parent's generation all remembered exactly where they were when they heard Pearl Harbor had been bombed. And I certainly remember where I was when I heard John F. Kennedy had been assassinated. Younger generations remember where they were on 9/11.

By summoning the memories of these important dates you can place the event into the context of your life.

That's important because everybody knows about the event itself, but they don't know what the impact was on you and the people you knew. Describing what you felt at the time you heard about it brings the event to life for people who didn't experience it.

What events should you choose?

First are public events that everyone knows about. These leap out at us from newspapers, historical timelines on the web, or history books.

Go through books focused on recent history and pick out the major events. How did they impact you? Your memories may be quite different from the public ones.

Think about politics, local or national.

Think about wars, riots, sporting events where records were broken, disasters, and so on.

How did they impact you?

This page of your writer's notebook is your opportunity to put into context for your readers how the broad impact of the outside world influenced your personal life.

Next, think about private events, or milestones in your life.

Where were you the first time someone asked you on a date?

When you first decided to move away from the home you grew up in as a child?

When you first decided to buy or rent your own home?

When you went on your first job interview?

As you chart your life, you are looking for these life-changing moments.

It might be helpful for you to have a conversation with the people you were with during those events. Ask them what other events are vivid to them. Then add your own impressions of those events, too.

Chapter 23

Childhood

In this chapter you'll begin to look at your childhood, and start creating entries for the Childhood pages in your writer's notebook.

Most of us don't remember being born (although my wife claims she does, but that's another story), however you probably know people who remember when you were born: siblings, parents, aunts and uncles, and so on. You can ask them about it if you're going that far back in your story.

Many autobiographies begin later in childhood, with early memories. What are your earliest memories of your parents? What kind of parents were they? What was your relationship like? What was their relationship with each other like?

In the Childhood section of your writer's notebook, include notes about your parents during that time—not your parents later in your life or as you relate to them now. That will help you really capture your childhood environment. Put yourself in the context of being a very small child and how your parents behaved towards you and what you thought about them.

Many children hold misconceptions about the way the world works, or their parents' place in it. My father was an engineer. When I was in grammar school, I thought that meant he drove a train. Did you have any misconceptions? When did you learn otherwise, and how did it make you feel?

If you had siblings, how did you get along with them when you were very young? Were you the youngest? Were you the oldest? Were you in the middle? Did they look up to you? Did they bully you? What was your relationship with them?

Think about the house you grew up in. For me there is no more vivid house in my memory than the one that I grew up in as a small child. I can tell you everything about that house. I know how the fibers in the carpet were woven, and the exact shape of the little moldings that ran around the bottom of the walls of my room. I can precisely visualize the heater vents, the shape of the doorknobs, the color of my closet door, and the way the paint chipped off of certain corners. Every detail of that house is still vivid in my memory.

Try sketching a floor plan of your homes; that's a great memory jogging tool. Think about what happened in each room.

Perhaps Aunt Bessie decided to change the drapes from yellow to purple in one room and it made the room much darker and then everyone felt different about it. Or the time that there was a leak in the family room and it got the table cloth all wet. Those are the sorts of anecdotes that can make a life story come to life!

We all have vivid memories about school. Do you remember your first day at school? Or that special feeling the first day of every year, when you might have been just a little excited even though summer vacation was over?

I have vivid memories of the playground. I was pushed down a couple of steps, broke my arm, and was driven to the hospital by one of the principals of the school. As we were leaving in her convertible she told one of the teachers she thought it was "B-R-O-K-E-N" as if, at seven years old, I didn't know how to spell!

What friends did you have at school? That's a fertile field for exploration!

What field trips did you go on? We went to the Hostess Cupcake Factory and the Wonder Bread Bakery when I was in grammar school. Every year those were our favorite field trips, because they gave us tiny souvenir loaves of bread to take home with us.

Think about vacations you went on when you were a small child. They were probably very different from the vacations you took later in life. Describe them from a child's viewpoint.

How about other outings? We went to Disneyland sometimes for birthdays. And we went to the local park for 4th of July picnics.

Did you like to play on the playing field or out on the playground at recess? Did you have a Merry Go Round, swings or a slide? Were you one of those kids who thought if you swung high enough and hard enough you could go over the top of the swing set?

What games did you like to play? Did you like board games, card games, outdoor games? I liked Life and Monopoly. My wife really liked Candyland, which drove her parents crazy. Did you play any of those board games?

Later on my parents taught me to play bridge and we would spend hours playing three-handed bridge. We also played poker, just for fun. What sort of card games did you like to play?

Were there video games when you grew up? When my daughter was young she loved immersive games like Myst, games about exploration and puzzle solving rather than action or fighting. Which ones did you like?

What were your favorite books, and why were they your favorites? Did you read them yourself, or were they read to you?

What movies or television shows had an impact on you when you were a child? Was there a really odd television show that only ran briefly and everyone else has forgotten, but was a favorite of yours? Why?

What are some activities you loved as a child, but no one would imagine you doing now? I was a competitive fencer in highschool! And I was a dance instructor at the Beverly Hills cotillion!

If sports were a big part of your childhood, be sure to share not just what you did but why you did it and why you liked it.

Also share your disappointments.

Is there something you used to love, but don't do anymore? Why did you stop doing it?

As you grew up, what material possessions were really important to you. Do you still have them? Perhaps a ring passed down from a grandparent. Or a junker car you saved up for by mowing lawns for many years? Make a list of such items, and add notes about why they were important.

Readers love to read about childhood experiences. See how many rich memories you can rediscover. In the next chapter we'll continue our exploration of childhood by revisiting our favorite toys.

Chapter 24

Toys and Possessions

When I think back on the toys I played with, it's inconceivable to me now. Those things were dangerous!

I had Lawn Darts, a Vacuform, Creepy Crawlers, and a lead soldier forge. That was crazy!

Lawn Darts were dangerous when used properly, and we used to throw them at each other!

The Vacuform melted plastic sheets over a red hot metal plate.

The Creepy Crawler machine cooked undoubtedly carcinogenic plastic goo.

And the lead soldier forge had a crucible where you melted down toxic lead bars and then poured the molten lead into molds you'd blackened with the soot from a candle.

What were my parents thinking?!

What were your favorite toys?

Did you play with blocks, Lincoln Logs, Tinker toys, Erector Sets, Chemistry Sets?

Did you have toys no one would dream of giving a child these days?

How did you feel about sharing your toys? Were you a child who freely shared your toys? Or were there special ones you kept for yourself?

Did you play with friends, or were you a loner? I was more of a solitary toy player. I'd build vast cities across the floor of my bedroom.

Try making a list of every toy you can remember, and put an asterisk next to your favorites.

Chapter 25

Pets

Pets can be our best friends, shape vivid memories, and star in great anecdotes. Particularly when we are growing up, pets can be a vivid part of our memories. Have you had pets in your life that were special?

As a small child did you expect pets to be more like humans?

Were there animals you were afraid of? Perhaps the neighbor had a pet that scared you?

Did you ever learn something from a pet?

Was there a time when a pet appeared to be smarter than the humans around it?

Those are all good subjects for anecdotes.

If a pet was very special to you, tell us all about it. Were you there when it was born? How did you first encounter it? What did it like to eat? What did it do that was unusual? How did it spend its days? If it has passed on then don't be afraid to talk about the sadness its death brought. That's a part of your experience, too.

Pets also can make good symbols in your story. Different types of people have different pets that often reflect their personalities. You can learn a lot about a person from how they react to pets.

If you talk to your pets, don't be afraid to include what you say as dialogue!

What is the strangest pet you ever had? My daughter had a bearded dragon that always got everyone's attention when they visited our house. Although we were skeptical at first, we grew quite fond of it.

People love to read stories about pets, because their own pets are special to them, so it's easy for them to understand and relate to yours.

Chapter **26**

Growing Up

What did you want to be when you grew up? I wanted to be a veterinarian. And before that an astronaut. And before that a collie.

I certainly never dreamed about being a theme park engineer or teaching writing to tens of thousands of students. It's funny what life has in store for us.

Think back to when you were very young. What did you want to be? Why did that seem like such a wonderful thing to become? How did it turn out? Did you end up becoming that, or along the way did life take some completely unexpected turns?

Put together a timeline showing what you wanted to be at various points in your life. How did you pursue those interests?

As a teenager your outlook on the world likely changed, and along with it your ambitions probably also changed. Did you exceed your original vision, or were there disappointments? How did you deal with each?

Develop other details of your life on that timeline as you moved from child to adolescent to tween to young adult and finally adult. All sorts of things can go on that timeline: first dates, first loves, first houses, first moves, first time out of the country, first car. Those are important events that can make great stories.

Tell us about your high school and college. Did you like school? And if not, why? If you did, what did you like about it?

Do particular teachers stick in your memory? Several teachers had a profound influence on my life.

Many people served in the military. If that's the case with you, it was likely an important part of your life. Tell us about it. What was it like at first? Was it hard to adjust? When you left were you relieved or did you miss it?

Tell us about your first jobs, other jobs, your career. Were they things you're passionate about, or simply a way to make money? Did you ever have unexpected trouble on the job or did anyone ever do something particularly special for you?

Looking at your timeline, which moments show a trajectory, show you growing and changing? Try to find some continuity. You might find several different threads running through that timeline that reflect your pursuit of goals. These will create a great narrative when you begin to assemble your manuscript.

Chapter 27

Accomplishments

As you think back on your life, you have many reasons to be proud of all you've accomplished. This chapter explores those feats, both major and minor. Be sure to make a note of each in the appropriate sections of your writer's notebook.

In school, did you get good grades? Were you recognized with any awards?

As you grew up, were you good at sports? Did you receive any awards?

At work, did you accomplish any special projects or receive any sort of commendations?

Have you been invited to speak to any groups?

Do you have any patents or inventions? Any publications?

What other things are you proud of in your professional or personal life?

These don't need to be major events. We're not necessarily talking about receiving the distinguished service cross. Perhaps some neighbors got together and threw you a surprise party. Or your family told you what a great job you'd done organizing a holiday dinner.

Have you thrown a great party, organized a trip, worked on a benefit? All of those are accomplishments worth talking us about, whether simple or complex. Tell us how you felt about the recognition people gave you.

Think about the proudest moments of your life. Now think about the struggle that led up to those moments, because if an accomplishment makes you proud you probably had to work for it. Now trace the history of those moments back, and show us how you achieved your goal.

Is there a relationship between these moments that made you proud? You can tell a lot about a person from the things they value most.

Chapter 28

Spirituality

Are you a spiritual person? Do you have deeply held religious or other beliefs? Are they beliefs you would like to share with others?

Your life story is a wonderful opportunity to explain to others what those beliefs are and why they are important to you. The values upon which your life is based can be reflected in nearly every paragraph you write. By showing others what you believe and why you believe it, you may be able to change their beliefs as well.

Many people who are spiritual go through a struggle that leads to an epiphany. They have a crisis and from its resolution they develop those deeply felt beliefs. That dramatic moment can inspire great storytelling. Think about the moments in your life when you were dejected and some form of spirituality helped you to recover and go on to greater success.

Just be sure your readers don't feel like you are preaching to them. It's more about showing them than it is about trying to convert them.

The best way to get someone to align with your views is to make them a sympathetic reader. And the best way to do that is to show them why it's important to you. Show them what you believe and how that belief came to be.

Even if you're not a spiritual person, you can still describe events in your life that you don't completely understand—things about your personality, your emotions, or things that are an unseen, a mysterious underlying layer of the world. Exploring the mysteries of life can make great reading.

Chapter 29

Holidays

For many of us, holidays are very special times. They a time of family joy, of gathering together, a time to reflect on the past year, a time to honor traditions.

Many of the traditions my family celebrates at the holidays are ones handed down for so many generations I don't necessarily know where they started or exactly what they mean. But I've had some joyous moments celebrating them with my parents and then with my own family and child. If you are the same, then holidays can be a wonderful source of material for your life story.

But holidays aren't happy times for everyone. Sometimes they bring sadness. If there have been times when you were disappointed or downcast during the holidays your life story should reflect that. And if there's something you learned from those times you can pass that on, too, in your holiday storytelling.

Different cultures have different holidays, and different holiday traditions. If yours are a little bit unusual, that's something your readers will enjoy.

For example, my family has a tradition that on holidays such as Christmas morning we make breakfast burritos together! I don't know if anyone else anywhere does that! It's something we started doing thirty years ago and it became a tradition. So now it's one of the things we look forward to. If you have something similar, be sure to share it with us so that we can temporarily become a part of your family.

One interesting way to write your autobiography would be to structure it as a meeting of family members getting together for the holidays. You could describe each different person as they arrive, and tell stories about them, one by one. You could also show how some of them have changed, and contrast their different personalities, or describe how they overcame obstacles to join their family for the holidays. It gives you a structure that makes storytelling easier, by creating a natural environment for a bit of conflict as everyone comes together. Remember that conflict in writing is a good thing, it makes interesting reading. And the most common form of conflict is dialogue. What better spot for some snappy dialogue than a giant family get together?!

In addition to holidays themselves, also consider incorporating the seasons into your life story. The seasons in many parts of the world are extremely different, and by capturing the weather, the changing hours of daylight, the change in the plants and trees, you can capture the feelings they evoke.

This can make your writing more vivid. When you set a scene in your story, if you establish the season it can have a lot to do with the feeling of that scene.

Weather is particularly useful. As previously mentioned, when characters in a movie are sad it's usually raining. Of course, sometimes reality runs counter to that. If it was a dark and stormy night when something wonderful happened, you may want to omit the weather, or take some artistic license and change it!

Whatever the weather in your part of the world, the holidays offer rich memories you can share with your readers.

Chapter 30

Romance

Romance is an important part of most people's lives. If you have a vivid memory of your first love, I'm sure your readers would enjoy hearing about it.

Did that love last? Or was it replaced? If so, what did you learn from that experience? What did you look for that was different later on? Or what did you learn from a lasting relationship that went on for many years?

I've been married to my wife for many years. Our relationship has in some ways remained exactly the same as it was on the first day we met, and in other ways it's changed. Those changes reflect how we have each developed, from teenagers to seniors. Readers will find that story arc very interesting.

Did you have a wedding ceremony? What was it like?

Do you observe anniversaries or other important dates? Have you surprised your love ones, or have they surprised you? Perhaps a bouquet of flowers or a gift that wasn't anticipated.

Are your relationships more oriented towards friendships? Do you have a large or small circle of friends? What makes a good friend? How do you treat friends, and how have they treated you?

Do your relationships involve a lot of sharing? If so, what do you enjoy sharing with your loved ones?

What intimate details are you willing to divulge to your readers? Such confidences can help them see you not just as the person you are now, but also the person you were at an earlier time. Don't be afraid to share those moments. It will make your past come alive. That's one of the things readers most enjoy in any autobiography. It enables them to see the humanness, and the vulnerability, and the potential for love.

Sharing those intimacies particularly helps bring your story to life for children or teenagers who might not easily be able to picture you when you were just like them. If you show them you shared those same passions they're now experiencing, they will see you in a new light. And perhaps they can learn from your experiences.

Chapter 31

The Black Moment

In every good fiction story, there is a black moment. It's the moment of deepest despair. It typically happens at the end of a long struggle, after a disaster. The character then makes some self-revelation that allows him or her to change and thereby succeed.

The black moment is a moment of absolute despair and hopelessness. I think most of us have experienced such black moments during our lives. One of your most unpleasant jobs in writing your life story is to include those moments. They are important. You mustn't convey the idea your entire life was a bed of roses. That would not only be dull, it would cheat your readers from knowing how you overcame adversity. Although it's painful, you need to address those dark times.

But don't just leave us in the black moment. Show us how you rose from the ashes, how you took defeat and turned it into victory. You're writing your life story; you're accomplishing something great. Show us how you overcame the adversities of your past and moved on.

What disasters have you experienced? Make a list of them, and how you recovered from them. Then decide which ones best fit into your story.

Revealing your black moments also serves to enhance what comes after, because of the contrast they provide. They are part of the ebb and flow of life.

Stepping back from some of your disasters now, you may have a little bit more perspective than you did at that time, and some of them might not seem so disastrous. Some things we thought were so important when we were teenagers don't seem quite that important in later life. I've seen some autobiographies where the writer has turned black moments into humorous incidents. That turns a black moment into a smile.

Chapter 32

Changes

In this chapter you're going to take a look at all of the changes in your life. So start a new page in your writer's notebook and get prepared, because lots of things have changed since the day you were born.

We all change jobs. Even if we've kept the same job our entire life, at some point we must have changed from not working to working. And it's likely you've had more than one job. Which jobs did you like and why did you like them the most? What was your first day like? Did anything funny happen to you as you were "learning the ropes"?

Another major change is moving. Have you moved state to state? Have you ever lived out of the country?

Do you have vivid memories of moving out of your parents' home? What was your first place like?

Try making a map of the different places you've lived. At maps.google.com you can create your own custom map that has markers for all of the different places you've been.

There are also sites that help you keep track of the different countries or states you've visited. How many are there? What's your best anecdote for each place you've lived?

What other sorts of transitions have you gone through in your life?

Have you had health challenges that caused changes in your life?

Have you made major changes in your peer groups, or the gang you hung out with. Why?

Do you have a mixed family that's the result of different marriages and divorces? That's probably very different from the environment you grew up in, so tell about those transitions.

Think about how technology has changed in your life. My goodness, it seems like technology is different from one month to the next. What was done very differently when you were younger? The tools I use to do my job—video recording with a phone, video editing with a computer, online education classrooms, on demand-publishing and ebooks —were undreamed of just a few years ago.

If you've lived longer than a few years then you've experienced a considerable change in technology. Describe to your readers how the world worked when you were a kid. What tasks were challenging then but we thought nothing of doing it that way, but are now done in an instant?

I remember when there were only a handful of television stations, you couldn't record television programs, no one owned a computer, exchanging letters took days or weeks, and if no one answered the phone you couldn't leave a message!

Are there technology changes that make some things harder to do now than they once were? For example, when you call a company to have a problem solved, is it harder to get someone to help you than it used to be, and if so why do you think that might be?

Other changes might relate to secrets you have kept. If you are ready to reveal any of those secrets, explain why you are now willing to share them with us.

What other likes and dislikes have you had in your life and how have those things changed?

Lately I find myself craving Brussels sprouts, something I hated when I was a kid. It's funny how our palates change as we grow older, and many of us prefer complicated flavors to simple sweets. How about you?

Think about moments where you made a choice and things could have gone in two completely different directions. What did you choose? And what do you think would have happened if you'd made the other choice? Do you have any regrets, or are you happy with the choices you made?

As you contemplate all the changes that have happened in your life, think about how you might connect them thematically. Explore how your choices combined to create the life you've lived.

Chapter 33

Children and Grandchildren

Now we'll turn our attention to one of my favorite topics: my brilliant child.

Just by saying that I've intimated a problem you need to avoid in writing your life story. We've all had the experience of someone pulling out a wallet full of photos and spending an hour telling us how brilliant their kids are, and all the things they're doing. It can get a little tedious. Because everyone's child is more brilliant than everyone else's child. And the grandkids are even smarter!

So when you write about children and grandchildren, instead of just talking about their accomplishments, talk about how they affected your own life. For any parent that's the most important thing. And your kids can write their own life story, later!

Describe the birth of your children, what it was like, what it meant to you. I'm sure you have some vivid memories of the time leading up to that special day. My wife was cooking Beef Bourguignon the night she went into labor.

And then bam! Life changes. What could change anyone's life more suddenly than having a baby that requires 24-hour attention?

After that first year or two it got a lot more fun. I loved watching my daughter develop.

It seems like they go from just toddling one day to running full tilt within a week or two.

And language: a first word, a few words, and then suddenly sentences. As speech develops, it's fascinating to hear children's thought processes now that they can communicate with others.

What childhood language stories do you have? When my daughter was two she used the word "yesternight." It's a marvelous word, and it got me wondering why it doesn't exist. It's very logical. If there can be yesterday, why not yesternight? It's a great example of the logical process of childhood speech development.

(By the way, I looked it up and discovered yesternight was coined by Shakespeare, along with a thousand other words we use every day, but for some reason that one didn't stick. Too bad, it's a perfectly useful word.)

How did your perspective change as a parent? Did you go from a happy go lucky existence before your child was born to one of playing the responsible figure of authority? Or were you the parent every other kid wished they had? I was probably the latter. I tended to explain alternatives to my daughter and let her make her own choices.

A nice way to structure an autobiography is to let it reflect the circle of life. You might begin with you as a small child, show how you grew and learned, and then passed the baton to the next generation, or even the one after that.

Be sure to ask your children and grandchildren what stories about you are important to tell. You might be surprised!

That brings us to the end of our brainstorming prompts, but it doesn't mean it's the end of your brainstorming. It just means your writer's notebook is now organized. You'll continue to add to all the topics as you prepare to write your manuscript, and even during the writing process. When something occurs to you, be sure to jot it down.

In the next chapter we're going to turn our attention to the techniques you'll use to bring your manuscript to life, to polish it, and ready it for publication.

Section 5
Your Manuscript

Chapter 34

Writing Big

As you write your manuscript, there are a few things you can do that will make it much better. It's easy to incorporate these techniques as you write, and they will save you editing time later.

Show, Don't Tell

We hear "show don't tell" all the time, but what does it really mean?

"Telling" is exposition. It's explaining something. It's what you might read in a history textbook. This is telling:

> We moved to Des Moines in the fall of 1984.

That's not very interesting. It doesn't bring a picture to life. It's just a fact.

But we could instead "show" our readers that move:

> The car wheels were noisy on the gravel of the road as we turned up the driveway of our new house in Des Moines. It was the fall of 1984.

That creates a scene in your mind instead of just telling you a fact. If you apply this technique to every sentence in your life story, it will be like watching a movie. It will captivate your readers. That's your goal.

Use Dialogue

Almost anything is more interesting to read with some dialogue mixed in.

If you find the pages of your manuscript are starting to look solid gray with typing, it's time to break it up and put in some dialogue.

For example, in the scene where we were rolling up the driveway in Des Moines, have the characters turn to each other and talk about the first thing they're going to do when they move into their new house. That will make it much more readable, and it affords you an opportunity to further develop the characters.

The Power of Suggestion

There are many opportunities to suggest things you don't need to go into long explanations about. For example, as we rolled up that driveway in Des Moines we talked about the sound of the gravel. That creates a mental picture of a cloud of dust coming out from behind the car as it goes up the driveway. I didn't actually mention a cloud of dust.

In fact, I couldn't really mention the cloud of dust. That's because the viewpoint character was looking forward, at the new house, not behind her. But even though I didn't mention the cloud of dust I suggested it using the sound of that gravel.

Look for these opportunities to use little bits of information to suggest far more than you actually include.

Metaphors

Metaphors—and their closely related cousins, similes—are ways to compare one thing to another. A metaphor says one thing is another. For example, if you say someone bats their butterfly wing eyelashes, you've turned their eyelashes into butterfly wings. On the other hand if you say her eyelashes are *like* butterfly wings, that's a simile. From a practical standpoint, they're almost the same thing.

There are lots of websites devoted to collecting great metaphors. Do a Google search for great metaphors and you'll find some you can borrow for your own writing.

Metaphors are a wonderful tool, as long as they're fresh. But when a metaphor is overused, it can become a *dead* metaphor. Dead metaphors are cliches. Here are examples:

> Avoid like the plague
>
> Dead as a doornail
>
> Like a kid in a candy store

We may use them everyday without thinking about them, but they stick out in writing. You should avoid them like the plague. Oops.

Symbols

I'm sure you've sat through high school English classes where the teacher found all kinds of symbols in a book and you wondered if the author really intended those to be symbols or they were just something the teacher invented. (Research has demonstrated it's usually the latter!)

But there are powerful ways to use symbols in your work.

We talked earlier about how weather can set the mood. That's a kind of symbol.

If you walk past a graveyard, that could create a sense of foreboding, and serve as a symbol for what's to come.

Even the sun shining could be a symbol.

Objects make good symbols. Perhaps an ancestor gives you a locket, and every time you are in crisis you clutch that locket in your hand. The locket becomes a symbol of hope, reinforced by its repeated use. When readers see you clutching that locket they will think, "Aha! She is experiencing a black moment, but she is hopeful, because she is clutching that locket."

Look for opportunities to incorporate symbols in your work, and to repeat them so that readers can glean their impact.

Make It Real

When you mention something in your manuscript, make it as real as you can. For example, don't write:

> There was a mailbox.

Instead, describe it:

> A rusty old mailbox sat on a post at the corner. The neighborhood stray dog used to sniff it every time he passed, looking for fresh messages.

Making it real means including some details, and showing it in the context of its use. It does not mean just stringing adjectives together:

> There was a rusty old blue dented mailbox.

That's not real, it's just cluttered.

***

So those are my techniques for writing big. If you apply them as you write, you'll end up with a much livelier manuscript, and you'll greatly reduce the amount of editing needed later.

Chapter

35

Writing Well

Now it's time to take your completed manuscript and polish it into something bright and shiny. That sounds like editing, and I suspect most people don't really enjoy editing. But I like it, because you can really see what you're accomplishing, line by line, as your rough drafts turns into something much more professional.

I'm going to show you some techniques that make editing lots of fun! They're simple to do and will make a tremendous difference in your finished manuscript.

Use Active Verbs

The first thing I'd like to suggest is that every sentence you write should be active rather than passive. There's a very easy way to accomplish that. Search your manuscript for the words "was" and "were," and see if you can find ways to replace those passive verbs with more active verbs.

Sometimes it's quite simple. Instead of

> "There was a bush in the garden."

you can write

> "A bush grew in the garden."

"Grew" is an active verb, "was" is a passive verb.

Instead of

> "There was a book on the table."

write

> "A book lay on the table."

There are also more dramatic ways you can transform your passive wording into active wording. Look for unexciting verbs about light or color or other states of being, and inject activity into your writing. For example instead of saying

> "Shade trees were planted along both sides of the road."

say

> "Shade trees canopied the road."

Often it's a matter of just switching around the words in the sentence. If you have written

> "There were shade trees along the road."

just switch them around and say

> "Trees shaded the road."

Notice how the revised versions are shorter. The side affect of using active verbs is that it will tighten up your manuscript. It's almost always a good sign when things get shorter.

Adjectives

The next suggestion I have is to use adjectives *well*, but *sparingly*. Many nouns can be improved by adding an adjective to make them more descriptive.

For example, we could talk about a book on the table or we could talk about a green book on the table. Or we could talk about a green leather-bound book on the table.

But you need to be careful about not over decorating your work. If you say there was a green leather-bound, rumpled, old, crackly, dusty book on the table, you've got so many words piled onto that poor book we've forgotten it was a book you were talking about in the first place.

So use your adjectives wisely. But do use them to bring your writing to life.

Adverbs

While adjectives are your friends, adverbs are your enemy. Stephen King has said, "The road to hell is paved with adverbs." Indeed, that is the case.

If you look at somewhat mediocre writing such as the popular *Twilight* series, you will discover reams of adverbs. Some chapters in that book have almost 200 adverbs. The shocking thing is, if you go through such a chapter and cross out all the adverbs and read back what's left, it doesn't make any difference. They're doing next to nothing. They're just being used to try to fix weak verbs. You can almost always find a more descriptive verb to use instead.

For example, instead of saying someone walked slowly, say they crept or they trudged or they plodded.

English is a rich language. There are so many synonyms with shades of differences. You can almost always find a better verb to replace one an adverb is trying to fix.

The quick way to find adverbs in your manuscript and eliminate them is to search for "ly", because most adverbs have that ending.

When you finish your manuscript, if you can state that there isn't an adverb in it, you can be proud.

Seen and Heard

Other things that are easy thing to find and eliminate are "senses" verbs. When you're in your character's viewpoint—and if you're writing an autobiography that probably means *your* viewpoint—you don't need words about the senses like "see" and "hear."

You don't need to say

"I looked out the window and I saw a car roll past."

You can just say

"Outside the window, a car rolled past."

We know you must have been looking out the window or else you wouldn't have seen and known to report that the car rolled past.

Similarly, you don't need to say

"I heard the clock strike twelve."

Just say

"The clock struck twelve."

The only way you could know is if you heard it.

It's superfluous to say "saw" or "heard." Search your manuscript for those words and find clever ways to eliminate them; they're just dead weight.

"That"

Another word that is really dead weight in most instances is the word "that." Some of us —and I fall into this category—are "that"ers. We tend to use a lot of "that"s. And most of the time the word "that" is just hanging around, doing nothing. If you'd like to check ~~that~~ for yourself, search your manuscript for the word "that." Cross it out, and see if the sentence doesn't mean exactly the same thing without it. I think ~~that~~ about three times out of four you'll find ~~that~~ it does.

Excess Verbiage

Another thing you don't need in your manuscript is excess verbiage. You don't need to talk about "the rosy fingers of dawn creeping above the horizon." Just say "the sun came up." We all know it looks pretty. If it was a pretty sunrise you can tell us what was pretty about it, but don't use overly florid language; it just makes your manuscript sound affected.

Clichés

Watch out for those clichés. They are a sign of lazy writing. But there is difference between a cliché in dialogue and a cliché in your expository writing. It's fine when you're capturing the way people speak to use the expressions they actually used in day to day speech. And a lot of those admittedly are clichés.

But when you're addressing the reader in your exposition you should avoid clichés. So don't talk about something being dead as doornail, just say that it's dead.

Coincidences

Avoid coincidences unless they really happened. And even if they *did* really happen, make sure there is some point to them happening before you mention them. Readers tend to associate coincidence with fiction, and you want them to believe what you've written is true.

In reality coincidences happen all the time. But in our writing they can be hard to believe. So unless the point of the anecdote is what an amazing coincidence it was, it might be best to leave it out.

Don't Dangle

Don't decorate your sentences with dangling participles. Participles (look for phrases containing "ing" endings) must be used carefully. Participles are used for a very specific purpose, they imply simultaneity. Don't write

> Opening the door, I went in.

That's impossible. You have to open the door and then go in. You cannot go in while you are opening the door. It doesn't work in the other order, either. You can't say

> I opened the door going in.

You have to do one and then other. So just say

> I opened the door and went in.

It is a common error of beginning writers to try to make their sentences seem more complex than they really are by attaching participles onto the beginnings and ends. But that doesn't really accomplish anything.

Some of the greatest writers, such as Ernest Hemingway, never wrote like that. They wrote short, declarative sentences that were easy to understand, and they used carefully selected nouns and verbs to convey their meaning.

That is what you should aim for in your writing as well.

***

If you follow the techniques I've described here, you'll be amazed at the amount of improvement you can bring to your manuscript in just a day or two of—I hesitate to say the word, but—editing. And maybe by the end of that process, editing will turn out to be one of your favorite things.

Chapter 36

Illustrations and Covers

Now that you've polished your manuscript, it's almost time to get it published. But there's a step you need to do first. You'll need to add interior illustrations and—if you're self-publishing—cover art.

Covers

If you are submitting your book to a conventional publisher, you can suggest what the cover might look like but you don't really have any control over it. Since the book is an autobiography or a biography, the publisher will probably be very interested in any artwork or photos you can provide to them to incorporate into a cover. But the actual design of the cover will be up to them.

On the other hand, if you are self-publishing through an organization such as createspace.com (which is owned by amazon.com) then you have complete control over what your cover looks like. Createspace.com makes it easy to design your own cover. You simply select a template, upload some photos or art, type in some text, and you're done.

You can also create camera ready art and upload it as your cover. You'll just need to take into account how wide the spine is, something that createspace.com will calculate for you when you upload your manuscript and select a book size.

If you're making your own camera ready cover art you'll want to include at least the title and author's name on the front. Most paperback books also carry a summary on the back cover. It should be a short and interesting description of what's in the book and why your potential reader should buy it. It could start with a brief excerpt from the book or just pose a question. The ISBN number and barcode also go on the back, but createspace.com will add that.

The best covers for autobiographies and biographies usually include one or more photos of the subject. Your cover could just be a photo, title and author's name, or it could be something more elaborate, such as a collage. Here's the cover I designed for a friend's autobiography:

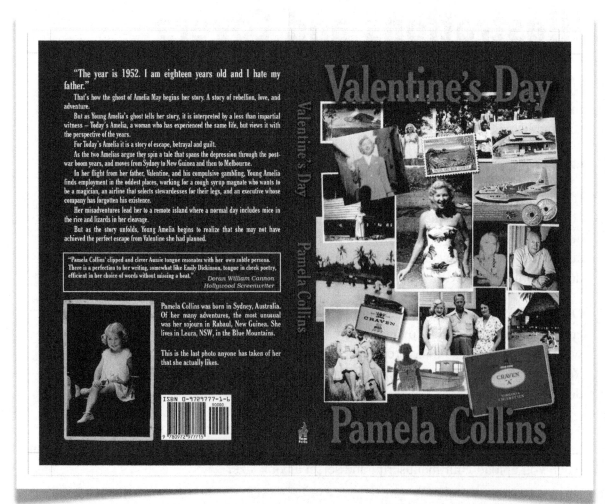

If you'd like a cover like that—or perhaps an illustration—it's easy to find graphic artists online who will create a cover for a modest fee. A great place to look for such talent is fiverr.com.

Some covers are simply typographic. It can be quite striking to get your message across using nothing but type. Here's one I did using only typography:

Another approach is to use a single photo. That's what I did with the cover of my memoir, *Building a Better Mouse.*

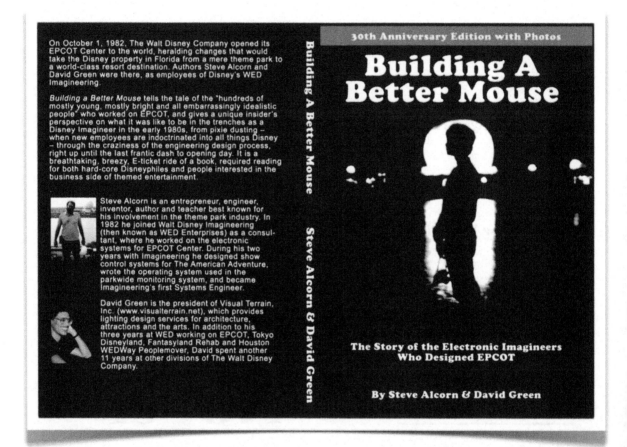

On October 1, 1982, The Walt Disney Company opened its EPCOT Center to the world, heralding changes that would take the Disney property in Florida from a mere theme park to a world-class resort destination. Authors Steve Alcorn and David Green were there, as employees of Disney's WED Imagineering.

Building a Better Mouse tells the tale of the "hundreds of mostly young, mostly bright and all embarrassingly idealistic people" who worked on EPCOT, and gives a unique insider's perspective on what it was like to be in the trenches as a Disney Imagineer in the early 1980s, from pixie dusting – when new employees are indoctrinated into all things Disney – through the craziness of the engineering design process, right up until the last frantic dash to opening day. It is a breathtaking, breezy, E-ticket ride of a book, required reading for both hard-core Disneyphiles and people interested in the business side of themed entertainment.

Steve Alcorn is an entrepreneur, engineer, inventor, author and teacher best known for his involvement in the theme park industry. In 1982 he joined Walt Disney Imagineering (then known as WED Enterprises) as a consultant, where he worked on the electronic systems for EPCOT Center. During his two years with Imagineering he designed show control systems for The American Adventure, wrote the operating system used in the parkwide monitoring system, and became Imagineering's first Systems Engineer.

David Green is the president of Visual Terrain, Inc. (www.visualterrain.net), which provides lighting design services for architecture, attractions and the arts. In addition to his three years at WED working on EPCOT, Tokyo Disneyland, Fantasyland Rehab and Houston WEDWay Peoplemover, David spent another 11 years at other divisions of The Walt Disney Company.

Building A Better Mouse

Steve Alcorn & David Green

30th Anniversary Edition with Photos

Building A Better Mouse

The Story of the Electronic Imagineers Who Designed EPCOT

By Steve Alcorn & David Green

I incorporated a photo that was taken during the events described in this memoir. And I tried to pick a photo that was a little ambiguous; I wanted readers to spend a moment figuring out what it was.

To illustrate your book you can't just do a Google search for images because most of the images that come up in a Google search are not in the public domain. They are owned by the person who put them on a website and you need to get permission to use them. Sometimes you can contact that person and ask them for permission to use their photograph. You could offer them a free copy of your book in exchange. You just need to make sure it actually is their photograph and not someone else's they used without permission.

But there are places on the web where you can get images you *are* allowed to use. They are stock photography sites. Most stock photography sites are in the business of selling stock photographs, but the good news is that you can purchase "royalty free" photos for a reasonable fee. The even better news is that many of the stock photography sites also offer free photographs in order to get people to come to their site and see what they've got.

Interior Illustrations

Of course you can use your own photos. If you're self-publishing, format your book using one of the interior templates offered at createspace.com and then paste the photos right into the manuscript file.

Try to find photographs that will reproduce very well in black and white on regular paper. It's extremely expensive to produce a book with colored photographs on nice glossy paper.

Including photos in your book might seem like a daunting task, but it's actually pretty simple, and it will make your book much more interesting.

Chapter **37**

Copyrights and Permissions

Before you turn that manuscript into a published book you need to check the copyrights and permissions.

Many students ask me how to copyright their work. You don't need to do anything but type the magic words on your title page. Modern copyright law says that anything you write is your own property. You don't need to fill out a bunch of forms or pay a fee. As soon as you publish your original words and you declare that you own the copyright, they belong to you. Just make sure that on the title page of your book you put a copyright notice, the date and your name. Either of these works fine:

© 2016 Steve Alcorn

(c) 2016 Steve Alcorn

But what about the copyrights on things that go into your book?

If you want to quote the lyrics of a song, you need permission.

If you want to include the contents of a letter someone sent you, you need permission. The person who wrote that letter owns it, even though they sent it to you.

There is something called "fair use doctrine" that allows you to quote small excerpts of other works, if you give credit. So, you could quote a couple of lines from a song or a couple of lines from a book or a letter as long as you credit the person who created them. That credit could be contained within the text where you introduce those lines, or it could be on an acknowledgements or copyright page where you list things you've included and the copyright holders' names.

If you want to use something longer you need to request formal permission and get it in writing. For songs or book excerpts you typically need to contact the publisher, although sometimes you can work directly with the author.

If that sounds like a hassle, well, it is a hassle. The easiest approach is to only use little snippets or just paraphrase the original.

You need to make sure your writing is all your own. It is fine to be inspired by other people's writing but it is not fine to copy their writing verbatim.

That applies to even short passages. If you copy a paragraph out of someone else's writing and you don't credit them as the author, that's plagiarism.

On the other hand, to be inspired by another autobiography and use its structure or format is fine.

Public figures and events that happened in public are fine to incorporate in your work. People don't own the rights to public information about their life. That is not true of private individuals, though. If you are revealing sensitive information about people in your book that others don't know, and if those people are still alive, you need to speak with them in order to get permission to use that information. However if the information is widely known and isn't libelous or scandalous, you probably can write what you like, with or without permission. But it's certainly better to obtain it.

Another approach is to change the names and claim the book is a work of fiction. That's what my friend Pamela did in her memoir, *Valentine's Day*. She changed every name in the book including her own and then claimed the entire book is fiction. We're left to decide for ourselves what is true and what is made up.

Once you've made sure you own everything in your manuscript, you're ready to publish. If you upload the manuscript to an on-demand publisher such as createspace.com, they will ask you to verify that you are the owner of all the material. If you've followed the process described in this chapter, you can answer with certainty, yes I am.

Now let's get that book into print.

Section 6
Publishing Your Work

Chapter 38

Getting into Print

This is the most exciting chapter, isn't it? Because now we're actually going to get you published.

Traditional Publishing

Traditional publishing used to be the only alternative. That meant finding an agent and finding a publisher.

If your book was accepted by a publisher, you would be given an advance, typically around $1500 to $5,000, but sometimes more. Your agent would take 15%.

And after a long period, usually a couple of years, your book would be printed with a press run of maybe 10,000 copies, and would be distributed to bookstores for a few months. Then the remainders would be returned from the bookstores to the publisher. You wouldn't have to give back any of the advance if the book didn't sell well, but few authors ever got anything beyond that advance.

The reason is that the royalty was only about 50 cents to a dollar per copy. By the time the unsold ones were credited back against the advance there usually wouldn't be any additional royalties.

That sounds like a lot of trouble to go to for a small amount of money. And your book wouldn't even be available at the bookstore anymore.

The picture is even worse, now, because there are so few bookstores left. Most books these days are sold through amazon.com. And a lot of them are electronic.

So, what to do? Fortunately, a tremendous technological advance has occurred in the last few years. It's called On-Demand Publishing.

On-Demand Publishing

It's important to understand that On-Demand Publishers are not Vanity Presses. Vanity Presses had a terrible reputation because they presented themselves as if they were publishers, but they were really printing companies. They wanted to sell authors a big pile of books that would live in their garage for the rest of their lives.

Vanity Presses would typically sell an author $5000 worth of books, delivered straight to them. They provided no distribution and they provided no marketing. In those days before the web there was no way for the author to sell those books other than grabbing a few of them and driving around town to bookstores and pitching them. So Vanity Presses had a real stigma attached to them.

Fortunately, On-Demand Publishers don't have any such stigma. Their business is to get your book into print. They only make money if your book sells because they're making money off of selling each copy. And the best On-Demand Publishers don't even charge upfront fees to get your book into print.

That means they're counting on you to sell your book. Yes I said that right, they're counting on you to sell your book. They are not going to market your book for you, you're going to have to find the market.

However even if your book were conventionally published these days by a big publisher, it is very unlikely that publisher would put any marketing dollars behind the book. They still expect the author to publicize the book.

That's why this book has a chapter on marketing. Because regardless of how your book is published, you will be the one making it sell.

Financially the difference is that you get no advance, but you make about $10 per copy sold. I don't know about you, but if I'm going to put the effort into selling a book I would much rather make $10 than 50 cents.

I highly recommend Amazon's createspace.com. Assuming you can do a minimum amount of formatting to get your manuscript into their template, there is no upfront cost to you. And you'll have the first copy of your book in your hands within a few days for just a few dollars. That's pretty amazing.

Do It Yourself or Get Help?

If you are completely new to word processing, if you don't understand anything about changing margins or page sizes or how headers or footers work, you probably need some help. But otherwise you can probably do this entire process yourself.

In the previous chapter I described how easy it is to create a cover using createspace.com. Creating the interior of the book is equally easy. You can download a Microsoft Word template for whatever size book you want and paste your manuscript into it. Or you can just format it yourself.

Look at a few other books to see what goes on to the title page and table of contents page. See what font they used and how they formatted the chapter breaks. Don't be afraid of having a few blanks pages in the front part of the book, blank pages or blank halves of pages are quite common. You'll quickly discover it's easy to turn out a nice looking book. Best of all, it will be yours. It will look exactly the way you wanted.

Uploading it to createspace.com is extremely straightforward. They will give you an ISBN number, something you'd otherwise need to buy.

They'll handle all the details of barcodes. They'll even check whether the formatting inside the book is correct.

If you're designing your own cover, they'll tell you how thick the spine will be. Or use their cover creator and it will all be taken care of for you.

If that all sounds pretty easy, it is. Give it a try, and if it's beyond your capabilities to do it, createspace.com has some people who will be happy to help you for a reasonable fee.

Within days you'll have the first copy of your book, for just a few dollars per copy. You can order a supply of them, and keep them in your trunk. Start distributing them to friends and family, take them to club meetings, sell them at book signings, donate them to auctions or libraries. We'll talk about all of this in the marketing chapter.

But first let's also make an e-book. It's just as easy. I'll show you how in the next chapter.

Chapter 39

E-books

In the last chapter we looked at how to turn your life story into a physical book. In this chapter we'll take a look at how to turn it into an electronic book.

E-books are now more than half of all books sold. There are so many people who have tablets and e-book readers that it's increasingly the way people read books. So, while it used to not be that important to have an e-book version of your book, now it is.

A nice thing about e-books is that if you are more interested in lots of people reading your book than in making money from it, you can price your e-book at free or very low cost and just give it away.

The easiest way to make an e-book, if you've publish your book through createspace.com, is to simply also use their conversion process to send the book right over to amazon's Kindle publishing division at the time you publish.

You just click on a box and it takes you over to amazon, you log in and the converted book is already there. Easy.

Now the bad news: It's almost impossible to control the interior formatting of Kindle books. You have little control over typography, spacing, or fonts. If you are trying to include tables or anything complicated in your book, it's a nightmare. Even making a clickable table of contents is a major project.

The reason for the difficulty is that as people change font or tablet sizes the pages flow completely differently. You don't have control over page breaks or margins.

You do have more control with Apple's iBooks publishing platform but it is significantly more complicated, you need a Mac to create one, and iBooks don't seem to sell as well as Kindle books. I published a version of my theme park design book on that platform and it looks fantastic. You can control everything about it and even embed multimedia files. I included sound recordings and all sorts of things in that edition. But it was a lot of work to create, and frankly the sales of that book haven't been particularly impressive because most people go to Amazon to buy their books.

Fortunately, you're writing an autobiography, so it's probably just a lot of text and some interspersed photos. That's fine for reading on a Kindle.

Another thing you can do at various websites is publish your audio or video. A little bit of web searching and comparing different customer reviews can turn up all sorts of different alternatives for publishing media yourself. I use amazon's acx.com to publish my audiobooks.

The web is truly a do it yourself paradise these days. Anything you can imagine, you can probably find a way to do.

***

I hope this quick introduction to Kindle book publishing has been helpful to you. If you would like to pursue it further, writingacademy.com offers an online course called *"Publish Your Book Now!"* that steps you through the entire process.

Now that your book is in print it's time to turn our attention to marketing!

Chapter **40**

Marketing

If you published your autobiography solely to share with members of your family and your friends, you can skip this chapter. But if you're passionate about sharing your life with others, this chapter will let you in on all my favorite marketing strategies.

Don't hide your light under a bushel! Let's take your book to the next level, get it out in the hands of readers and share your wisdom, your life, your experiences.

These are things that have worked for me.

Speak at Schools, Clubs and Libraries

Libraries are a terrific location because you will meet strangers who've come because they saw an author was going to be there to speak. The library staff will be happy to set that up for you.

Always have your books available for sale. Sell them for a nice round number like $10 or $20 so it doesn't require a lot of change.

And always make sure you have a pen so you can offer to autograph the books. That's a big selling point for many people.

When you autograph your books, do it on the title page. Ask the buyer whether they would like it to be personalized to a specific name.

Add a message like "Best Wishes" or "Happy Reading."

Press Releases

Write a press release for your book and send it to anyone you think would print it. Local newspapers are the best bet; big city newspapers probably won't. Local newspapers are always looking for material to fill their editorial pages.

If you belong to clubs or a homeowners association that sends out newsletters, make sure they get a copy of your press release.

In the press release describe what inspired you to write the book. It's that human interest aspect that will get it run.

Also be sure to mention how people can obtain the book. If it's available on amazon.com (as it will be if you publish it through createspace.com) then tell them the book is available on amazon.com and they can search there to find it.

Bookstores

Bookstores love to host authors. Unfortunately there aren't very many bookstores anymore.

It doesn't matter if the store carries your book. You can just take a box with you, the store will ring up any that are sold, and then pay you your cut, which is usually 50%. You take the unsold books home.

It's not an easy way to make a living. It's a long day. But if you schedule a reading you'll do much better. People are more likely to gather when there's a group listening to a speaker.

If you're a good reader and you tell an interesting story you'll catch their attention and they'll want to meet you and perhaps buy a copy of your book.

The store will give you a table where you can have a stack of books to sign after you read. But if you just sit at that table with the stack of books you will not sell any. Make an effort to engage people in conversation. If you make eye contact you will sell some books.

Take a couple of friends with you. Those friends will look like they're already customers chatting with you, so make sure they don't position themselves behind your table or engage in very personal conversation with you. Make sure the way they stand and the way they talk with you is as other customers would.

Book Fairs

Book fairs are full of people who are receptive to learning about your book. The purpose of these events is to expose new authors to the public. You have to buy a table at these events. It can run from a few dollars to hundreds of dollars. If it's on the high end, it can be a challenge to break even.

You spend the day sitting at the table talking with the people who come by, signing copies for those who wish to purchase.

If you pick an event that has a theme related to what your book is about it can be more successful. For example, books about town history sell well at history themed fairs.

Website

A website is really important for promoting any book. It used to be hard to set up a website but now it's easy using wordpress or blogger or wix.com. If you don't mind a few ads on your site, you can probably do this for free.

For a slightly more professional approach you can register your site name with a web registrar such as GoDaddy and they host your site for a small monthly fee. Their site building tools are pretty easy to use.

A good name for your site or blog is either the author's name or, if you plan to only write one book, the book name.

If you create a blog you need to keep it up to date. Post at least once a month. Once a week is better.

Bookmarks

Many authors print up bookmarks with an ad for their book and give them away. The bookmark can include a picture of the cover, a sentence about the book, and a link to purchase it on amazon.com.

That is cheap advertising!

Advertising

Speaking of advertising, I haven't had very much luck with magazine advertising or paid advertising on the web. But you can get free editorial coverage by writing a story (or just using an exciting excerpt from your book) for local publications or even national magazines. You might even get paid for the content! At the end of the excerpt you can tell people where they can get a copy of the book.

Charity Auctions

Here's one that's interesting to me and I haven't heard of many authors doing it. Donate a book to a charity auction. One autographed copy of your book on the silent auction table with a retail price of $20 is likely to get a bid of $20.

That's great, you did a good deed.

But whether it sells or not, all of the people at the auction saw your book. They read the description, they saw the cover, and some of them will remember it and maybe even buy it later.

Internet Author Sites

You can create a free author's page at amazon.com. Then you claim all of your book titles and they'll be listed on your page. Visitors who look at any of your books can click a link that will take them to your author page where they will find all your other books. You can also post information there and can link to your blog.

If you don't belong to goodreads.com you should join. It's a great way to keep track of all the books you've read by placing them on virtual bookshelves. It's easy to find recommendations from people who like the same books you do.

And as an author you can claim your books on goodreads and carry on a dialogue with your readers and potential readers. It's a great way to publicize yourself.

Radio and Podcast Interviews

This next one is a little bit more difficult because it requires you to have a topic that interviewers think would be interesting to their listeners. I've bought many books after hearing the author being interviewed.

If you search the list of podcast topics or radio programs related to your subject matter, you might be surprised at how easy it is to get booked. And don't restrict yourself to just local shows. They could be anywhere, because these interviews are typically done over the telephone, or via Skype.

Contests

There are two ways to promote your books using contests. One is by entering contests. I'm not a fan of that approach. I don't think it gives you much visibility, and often there is an entry fee, so the contest is really just a business.

The second way is to donate books as contest prizes. This works much better. It gives your books similar exposure to the auction technique. The best place to donate books is to blogs about reading where book prizes are offered. A Google search will turn up hundreds of them.

Carry Books With You

Always carry books with you. You cannot sell books if you don't have them. Keep some books in your car's trunk. When you go on vacation throw some copies into your luggage.

When people ask what you do, tell them, "I write books."

They'll ask, "What about?"

After you tell them, they are likely to say, "I'd be interested in reading that."

Your response can then be, "I have a copy in my car if you'd like to buy one. I'd be happy to autograph it for you."

It's hard to say no to that offer!

***

Every writer is different, and what works best for you will depend upon your personality. It's worth trying many different approaches until you hit on the magic combination that works for you.

Chapter 41

Next Steps

Thanks for joining me on this exciting journey. It's been quite a trip hasn't it? We've explored every aspect of crafting your life story including structure, writing techniques, memory prompts, manuscript polishing, getting into print and marketing.

I hope you've enjoyed it, and I wish you great success writing your life story. It's a wonderful gift to share with family, friends, and future generations. They will thank you for it.

If you've enjoyed this book, please review it on amazon.com. It helps our sales, and it will help your sales if you ask your readers to do the same for your book!

I'd like to invite you to visit us at writingacademy.com, where you'll find online classes in many topics, including a video version of this book where you can ask me questions and get my help in developing your story. We also have a class that steps you through the publishing process. It's called *Publish Your Book Now!*

I hope to see you online, and I look forward to receiving my very own autographed copy of your life story.

Until then, Happy Writing!

About the Author

Steve Alcorn is the CEO of Alcorn McBride Inc., a company that designs products used in nearly all of the world's theme parks. He is the author of many books, including historical fiction, romance, young adult novels, and the non-fiction books *How to Fix Your Novel, Building a Better Mouse* and *Theme Park Design.*

During the past decade he has helped more than 30,000 aspiring authors structure their novels through the online learning programs of 2000 colleges and universities worldwide. Enroll at http://writingacademy.com

Follow him on Facebook at https://www.facebook.com/WritingAcademy

Sign up for the Writing Academy Newsletter at https://writingacademy.com/pages/about to receive free writing tips.

Made in United States
Orlando, FL
07 April 2022

16602028R00091